A TOOTH IN MY POPSICLE

And Other Ebullient Essays on Becoming Filipino

David Haldane

Black Rose Writing | Texas

ISBN: 978-1-68513-111-1
PUBLISHED BY BLACK ROSE WRITING
www.blackrosewriting.com

Printed in the United States of America
Suggested Retail Price (SRP) $19.95

A Tooth in My Popsicle is printed in Garamond Premier Pro

*As a planet-friendly publisher, Black Rose Writing does its best to eliminate unnecessary waste to reduce paper usage and energy costs, while never compromising the reading experience. As a result, the final word count vs. page count may not meet common expectations.

To my wonderful children,
Isaac, and Adira,
who made this journey worthwhile.

A TOOTH IN MY POPSICLE

AUTHOR'S NOTE

These are stories of transformation.

When my Filipino wife, Ivy, and I conceived the idea of moving to the Philippines in 2008, the decision was driven by desperation. Life had changed in America, especially for victims of what—in the days prior to COVID-19 and its aftermath—we called the "mother of all recessions." I was one of them; after twenty-three years as a *Los Angeles Time* staff writer, I walked into the newsroom one day and was told to turn right around and march back out.

Two months later, Lehman Brothers—the fourth largest investment bank in the United States—declared bankruptcy and America's then-worst economic downturn since the Great Depression had officially begun.

It was in that environment the idea of escaping to the Philippines reared its promising head. My beautiful wife was from there. She had a vast family and lots of connections. Life on the islands looked simpler. And so, our dream took flight.

It would be a decade, however, before it finally landed.

This collection of personal essays begins a few months prior to our eventual departure, as Ivy and I plan the renewal of our wedding vows in the small thatched-roof village of her birth on Siargao Island, the now-famous surfer's paradise in northeastern Mindanao. It ends just over two years later with the entrance of our newborn daughter in the house we built overlooking Mindanao's historic Surigao Strait.

By then the world was struggling amid a global tragedy nobody had foreseen—the devastating coronavirus pandemic of 2020—as we welcomed our first child born on the soil of the strange new world we had adopted as our own.

What began as a blog for a now-defunct website called *Live in the Philippines* eventually morphed into "Expat Eye," a weekly column for *Mindanao Gold Star Daily*, one of the leading newspapers in the sometimes-troubled region we now call home. Some of these essays, especially the earlier ones, draw on experiences gleaned during the many trips we took to the Philippines before moving there. Together they tell the story of a transformative adventure, sometimes frightening, often frustrating, occasionally hilarious, but always, I hope, entertaining.

They could also be of some value to those who, for whatever crazy reason, may one day choose to follow.

David Haldane

January 2023

1
RENEWING THE VOWS

March 21, 2018

It began as a promise.

Asking a young woman to leave the deep provinces of the Philippines for a new life in America is asking a lot. Abandoning her family and friends, possibly forever, she is entering a new world, one usually devoid of anything familiar; an environment less like the one she knows than almost anything imaginable. What you are asking her to do is trust you—someone she probably just met—to provide for her, protect her and guide her into an unforeseeable future fueled by the vague notion that *your* world will one day be *hers*.

You are also asking her to forgo something she may have fondly imagined since childhood: a real wedding.

We got married in a little chapel outside Las Vegas. It wasn't bad; though not actually Catholic, it had all the trappings. And though no one she knew attended, four of *my* friends were present; two American men and their Filipino wives who had made this journey before her.

Still, I sensed a quiet uncertainty in my bride's soul. It was present as we nervously watched the clock, eager not to exceed the allotted time and cramp the wedding after ours. It showed in her eyes as we said our vows, a look of subtle bewilderment and desperation. But there was something else there too, a faith in the universe, the innocent expression of someone who believes all is as it should be and everything will turn out fine. I made a silent vow of my own then; that my dear love's faith would not go unrewarded.

"Honey," I whispered in her ear, "don't you worry. One day, we will do this right."

That was ten years ago. Now the time has arrived to fulfill that whispered promise; soon we shall renew our vows in the land that is her sustenance.

Ivy hails from a small teardrop-shaped island in northeastern Mindanao, a place called Siargao in the province of Surigao del Norte. Famous for its white-sand beaches and world-class surf, Siargao was a sleepy little-known paradise when I first encountered it more than a dozen years ago. Later, travel bloggers, developers and tourists discovered the island. A popular feature-length movie bearing its name recently opened in Manila, and today the island has become something of a playground to the stars.

At least one spot, though, retains the innocent charm of the lazy place that once coaxed me into loving it as I do my wife. It is the *barangay*, or small neighborhood, of Caridad, a tiny thatched-roof village on the island's eastern shore where the laughter of wide-eyed children wafts daily in the waves. It is on this beach that my beloved once frolicked as a girl. And it is on its sand that I will marry her again.

Our planned wedding promises to be the grandest event of Caridad's year. We have fashioned a long list naming the sponsors, flower girls, relatives, and friends who will lead our parade. We have hired the services of a real Catholic priest, ordered Hawaiian shirts for those who don't own *barongs* (the fancy embroidered shirts Filipinos wear on formal occasions) and fattened five pigs to feed the entire town.

Now it's my turn to feel nervous as Ivy makes the final preparations. But just as she once gifted me with her faith, so will I now gift her with mine. Thus, on a certain Saturday in April, within days of our 10th anniversary, we shall stand on Caridad beach repeating vows as our seven-year-old son, Isaac, bears new diamond rings.

Strange how, as a foreigner, I feel so rooted to this place. If you are anywhere near, we hope you will come.

2
MARRIAGE ENGRAVED

March 29, 2018

I spent most of yesterday typing.

It's a job to which I am accustomed. As a newspaper reporter for over three decades, typing was my daily bread and butter. Now, working at a small radio station in Southern California, I still perform the task with a fair amount of frequency and speed. One could say that typing and I are old acquaintances.

Fairly new, however, is the typing I did yesterday, namely the typing of lists. Specifically, exceptionally *long* lists. The lists of participants in our upcoming renewal of nuptials in the Philippines. For readers with limited patience and time, let me quickly summarize; what we're talking about here is over 90 names divided into 14 categories.

A partial list of the categories involved might be instructive. There are the usual ones including *best man, maid of honor, groomsmen,* and *bridesmaids.* Add to that a few categories less familiar to those unschooled in Philippine marital culture, such as *primary* and *secondary sponsors; to lay our symbol of love and commitment; to light our path;* to *clothe us as one, to bind us as one; to carry our symbol of love; to carry the Holy Bible; to carry our treasure;* and *to carry the cord.*

Perhaps you can appreciate my consternation. And that's not even the guest list, which I haven't yet seen.

I don't presume to understand all those functions, nor the significance they play at a wedding. What I *will* say is this; you haven't really experienced a wedding until you've been to a *Filipino* one. Or, in our case, the mere *renewal* of a wedding. What does all of it mean? Simply that in a land where divorce is illegal, well, the damn wedding better impress.

I've heard all the arguments, of course, regarding the alleged backwardness of the fact that the Philippines is virtually the world's only country still banning divorce. It oppresses people stuck in intolerable relationships by forcing some to abandon their families while others stay unwillingly with theirs. And, perhaps worst of all, it enshrines the power of the Church in a developing country taking halting steps into modernity.

At the risk of sounding hopelessly reactionary, however, let me just say this; I find something comforting in this pro-marriage stance. In a universe increasingly bereft of lifelong commitments to *anything*, let alone another person, it is oddly refreshing to encounter even the symbology of a stance against divorce. And though I recognize its likely demise in the face of rational argument, that is not an outcome I celebrate.

All that said, I am not the poster boy for lifelong fidelity to marriage. Truth be told, the decade-long union we will soon commemorate before that grand mass of well-wishers on Siargao Island is not my first, but my *third* such union. Hopefully and predictably, it will also be my last. And there lies the irony; that only by navigating the fiery coals of divorce have I finally learned to value the cool embrace of marriage.

None of which, naturally, makes any difference to the Catholic priest who recently informed us that, because of my sordid marital history, he cannot officiate at our upcoming renewal of vows. We have appealed that decision on the grounds that next month's ceremony will not be an actual wedding, but the *renewal* of an existing one already long consummated and legally sanctioned. If that fails, we can always go to the mayor.

Perhaps he will be the one to *carry the cord* that will *bind us as one*.

3
ALL IN THE FAMILY

April 12, 2018

It started as a gag.

Ivy and I, happily married, would fantasize about whether some of her female relatives might be up for similar marital unions. What fueled the fantasies, of course, was the well-known and often remarked-upon Filipino penchant for taking care of their own.

"When will you find a husband for your sister?" somebody would remark, only half in jest. Or, "Surely you won't leave your cousin behind?"

From our own family nest in Southern California, such pleas seemed far-fetched, though admittedly romantic. So we indulged them as best we could. "Who do we know that's single, eligible, and male?" I'd ask Ivy in a rhetorical exchange often accompanied by a wink.

One night we were sharing drinks with my best friend from high school, now a retired English professor, when his wife, Bonnie, blurted out something that seemed fitting for the occasion. "You guys are so happy," she declared, looking at Ivy and me. "We should find someone for Jesse."

Jesse was their good friend, a single guy in his late forties who Bonnie had kind of adopted as a stand-in son.

"Hey Ivy," she continued, "don't you have a *sister*?"

Everyone laughed with a heartiness befitting the amount of alcohol we had consumed. Then stopped. "Actually," said Ivy, "I *do*," and so the project began.

At first, we just gave them each other's email addresses. They talked from opposite ends of the ocean. Then came the questions. Was Jesse a good man, she wanted to know, and would Ivy's sister, Kiking, be loyal? How well did we really know this guy? Gradually, the tenor changed; How long would it take to process her visa and when would she be able to work? And, finally, the tasks became more concrete; we helped him buy an airline ticket for the required trip to meet her in person.

Through it all, the four matchmakers periodically got together over drinks, gleefully comparing notes. Though none of us believed the relationship would go anywhere, we were certainly enjoying the ride. When Jesse returned from the Philippines, however, there was a definite new sparkle in his eye. "We're in love," he announced almost immediately. "We're gonna get married and have lots of kids." And so, it eventually came to pass that Jesse is my brother-in-law, and Kiking calls California home.

In fact, Ivy's sister isn't the only one for whom we've enabled immigration. We also helped her first cousin find a mate and petitioned for both her parents to come over and join the fun. In the decade since our marriage, I would guess that we've been at least partially responsible–either inadvertently or by design–for perhaps a dozen new Filipino immigrants to America, mostly through encouragement and advice. I suppose you could call us a regular Filipino/American immigration service, though in the current political climate I'd prefer that you didn't.

But here's the irony; just as our friends and relatives get settled here, we are preparing to leave. We've already arranged for Ivy's sister and her new husband to occupy our cozy desert home in Joshua Tree, California, after we move to the Philippines this summer. Ivy's cousin is well on his way to landing a permanent green card and embarking on a healthcare career. Soon, they will have to fend for themselves. Because it's a revolving door. And once we've passed through it, well, *we'll* be fending too.

4
THE THING ABOUT POOP

April 19, 2018

There's something about poop that makes Westerners nervous. Though I can't say exactly what it is, I know this; most Filipinos do not share the discomfort.

That was first driven home to me last year during a brief sojourn in Dapa, the teeming port city on the southeast corner of Siargao Island. We were just passing through, really, on our way to the island's interior, when nature placed an urgent call. While I might ordinarily have answered with a pleasant hello and perhaps a short chat, it immediately became apparent that, on this particular day, nature was in no mood for pleasantries.

So, I consulted my wife, who immediately directed me to the nearest public restroom. And there lay the rub; placed demurely at a table, directly blocking my path, sat one of the loveliest young ladies I'd ever seen. "Yes, sir," she said brightly, with a heart-stopping smile. "Five pesos or ten?"

It soon became apparent that what she was referring to was the exact nature of my business. While five pesos would get me past her with mere zipper rights, only ten would guarantee any privileges beyond that; duly enforced, I gathered, by her possession of what appeared to be the only toilet paper in town.

Even as I inwardly rejoiced at my complete comprehension of her question, however, my very soul rebelled at the idea of sharing the intimacies of my bathroom needs with this complete—and worse, *attractive*—stranger.

"Uh, how much just to go in?" I timidly inquired.

"But sir," she shot back with what I imaged to be a barely discernable wink, "will you be needing the paper?"

That's when I realized there was no escape. She had me trapped. Without another word, I nodded, handed over the ten pesos, and held my hand out for the much-needed sanitary material. "Is this enough?" she persisted, offering a strip of tissue thin enough to be ripped to shreds by my increasing hyperventilation. "Or do you need *more*?"

It was the closest I've ever come to fainting. The second closest came fifteen minutes later when I ventured back out that door to bathe in her radiant smile as she bid me good day. "Come back soon," she said cheerfully, like a saleslady at the mall. I just cringed and slunk away.

There was another time my self-imposed shame and the biological necessities of the human condition conspired to ruin my life. It happened more than a decade ago at Magpupungko Beach, the now-famous stretch of sand on Siargao Island where my wife's family owns property. It was almost devoid of structures back then, the perfect place for a family picnic during our "getting acquainted" period, otherwise known as courtship. Everyone was there: Mom, Dad, several siblings, aunts and uncles, nephews, nieces and, of course, the usual swarm of cousins. So it was with some shyness that I leaned over to gingerly whisper in my sweetheart's ear; "hey, honey, where's the restroom?"

Her look of astonishment filled me with dread. "Babe, I don't think there's anything like that on the beach," she said, obviously trying to break it to me gently. There followed a long discussion in their native language of *Bisaya*, not a word of which I understood. And, as each relative took a turn speaking up in what had clearly become a full-blown family discussion, well, my dread quickly turned into catatonia.

"Sweetheart," my fiancé finally announced, no longer even bothering with the pretense of a whisper, "we'll just have to find you a tree. Kindly come with me."

I remember extraordinarily little of what happened after that. She must have taken my hand and led me dumbly through the field of coconut trees. At some point, she probably identified a worthy one and explained what was about to happen. I have a vague memory of her standing guard before leading me back to the family gathering. And a far more vivid one of the family's all-around knowing smiles.

Later—in my honor, I suppose—they erected a small comfort room near the spot, exceedingly crude and made of stone. Though it has since crumbled into oblivion, I still cringe at the sight of the old rock pile where that restroom once stood.

It's been years since my humiliation at the beach, and now we're building a house in the very same province. Besides air conditioning, I have only one unconditional demand: American-style toilets. Flushing ones. With seats. And lots of toilet paper within easy reach.

Oh, and one other thing; securely locked doors to conceal it all.

5
LIGHTING UP THE SKY

May 3, 2018

It was the first time Caridad Beach had ever seen fireworks.

We hadn't exactly planned it that way. But, in envisioning the renewal of our nuptial vows on the beach where my wife had romped as a child, a wedding planner asked whether we wanted to light up the sky. Ivy and I looked at each other and, realizing we were already way over budget anyway, shrugged our shoulders and said, "why not?" And so it happened that myriad-colored sparks erupted on a recent Saturday night over the white sands of Siargao Island. What had begun as a promise had become a reality: our tenth anniversary emblazoned in lights.

To make that happen, of course, required a great deal of preparation. Our wedding planners had assigned processional titles and printed up programs. We had completed travel plans for ourselves, as well as guests from afar. Ivy had selected color schemes and rented dresses. And dozens of bridesmaids had squeezed into the handful of beds in a single house with one bathroom and no running water. Only then came the last hurdle; a nail-biting conference with the grim parish priest to convince him we would not be violating any cardinal rules.

As per his instructions, the festivities began the next day with a Thanksgiving Mass in the local chapel. Then retreated to the beach for the custom-designed ceremony followed by a long night of carousing.

The event was not without its glitches. The master-of-ceremonies had neglected to remind us to write our own vows, forcing us to do some quick ad-libbing. And when Ivy and her bridesmaids performed the dance they'd been practicing all week, the host overruled my impassioned objections to insist on my unrehearsed participation. The result: a group of smart-prancing performers moving in slick unison accompanied by a lone *barong*-clad white guy up front resembling a cheap marionette attached to the strings of a drunken puppeteer.

Ah, but then came the fireworks, and all was forgiven. A few hundred souls spontaneously jumped to their feet in a gut-wrenching cheer. And as the disco music ground deafeningly past the edges of a wind-wisped night under the salt-scented trees, I knew instinctively that everything had turned out fine. In fact, it was perfect. Later, the barangay captain, clearly emotional, sought me out to say thanks. "This is important for Caridad," he said, gripping my arm, almost weeping with joy. "So many people. So good for the community..."

His was one of many expressions of gratitude that night.

And that's how I learned something new about my wife's home country. Everyone who's ever been to the Philippines knows of its penchant for partying. What fewer understand, though, is how deep that really goes and what it says about the culture's equal penchant for reverence and gratitude.

For what began at the church had spread to the beach. Thank you, I thought, for this most amazing moment. Thanks for the ocean and the moon and the stars. Thanks for the fireworks that lit up the sky. Thanks for this marriage that has lasted these years. And thanks for this place that has inspired joyful tears.

6
LOST AND FOUND

June 7, 2018

It felt like I'd taken a pill and suddenly realized it was the wrong one. Instant panic erupted in me like a surge of vomit from my gut. "Oh my God," I thought, "I've lost my bag."

It was a balmy night in a town called General Luna, the beating heart of Siargao Island. By then I'd grown accustomed to carrying the little gray bag slung neatly over my shoulder. In it was my wallet, containing a driver's license, credit cards, and small amount of cash. Losing all that, of course, would constitute a major problem. But that wasn't even the worst of it; I'd also stuffed several important legal documents into the bag's side pocket, including my passport. "This is a calamity," I screeched at my still-unperturbed wife. "We need to retrace our steps!"

When that failed to turn up any clues, we stumbled numbly into the local police station to fill out a report. I did not know how or where I'd lost my bag. My best guess: that I'd stuffed it into one of the side panels of our car from which it had escaped through an open door.

But we were on Siargao to renew our wedding vows and so I kept my cool. Anyone who's ever misplaced a wallet, especially in a foreign country, can appreciate the sense of helplessness it engenders. You feel weightless, as if the next gust of wind will blow you away. Ah, but I was with my calm island wife, who helped me swallow my fears. Nothing to do, we decided, but try to forget about it and enjoy the rest of our stay.

The day after our wedding ceremony on the beach–and four days following my loss–we hired a pump boat to take twenty guests on an island-hopping tour. I had just clambered aboard at its berth in Dapa when a dark-haired young woman, apparently the skipper's aide, smiled and asked me my name. "Did you lose your bag, sir?" she inquired, and it was as if God's hand had burst out of heaven and grabbed me by the collar.

The upshot: someone had found the bag and given it to his son, who operated a fruit stand in town. He, noting the name on the driver's license, had placed a notice on Facebook. The boat owner, recognizing the name as one of his paying customers, had responded. And *voila!* The lost bag was found.

To make a long story short, we rushed back to General Luna where, at a place called *Jolan Fruits and Vegetables*, I finally enjoyed a reunion with my long-wandering bag. Much to my relief–and, I must sheepishly admit, *surprise*–everything was still intact, including the documents and cash.

We gave the guy a reward, of course, and promised to donate to his favorite charity. So what have I learned? Good people exist everywhere, including on the shores of remote poverty-stricken islands. Fanny packs are safer than shoulder bags. And, finally, the utterly astounding karma I've experienced related to everything involving the Philippines seems to continue.

My conclusion: apparently God really does want me to move here.

7
HOUSTON, WE'VE GOT A ROOF

April 5, 2018

The roof is red.

The color is no surprise, as we picked out tiles of that hue. And it's not surprising either that, against the backdrop of blue ocean and green coconut trees, the red roof looks striking. No, the genuine surprise is that there's anything there at all.

We planned it that way, of course. But planning is one thing and *seeing* another. The bottom line: after years of fantasizing, we finally see something resembling a house.

Before going on, I should probably explain. The thing resembling a house is at a place resembling paradise. Ivy and I discovered it four years ago when a friend and former classmate of hers, hearing that we sought land, steered us to the spot. It's called *Punta Bilar,* which, in the local vernacular, means Point Watch. And never was a place better named.

Perched at the very tip of a peninsula jutting like a finger above Surigao City, it is literally the furthest north you can get and still be in Mindanao. There's a road there, and green hills, and fabulous views of the ocean with verdant islands in the distance. And right next to the hill on which our home will one day perch, sits a white lighthouse complementing the fluffy white clouds like a shepherd watching sheep.

The first time we stood on that hilltop, it was as if we had come to an intersection in time; a mystical point at which past, present, and future magically converged. "This is it," I whispered to Ivy, squeezing her hand. "I think we're home."

And so came the day when, after the ritual signing-of-the-papers, we convened at a local bank with the farmer selling the land. "Would you like a check or electronic transfer?" I asked the stooped gent, sporting a toothless grin.

"Oh sir," he said, "please cash only."

So the bank's petite female manager disappeared into its vault for what seemed like an eternity. Then re-emerged hauling, with some difficulty, a satchel full of money. The old man, never skipping a beat, opened a shopping bag, accepted the 1.5 million pesos the bank manager dumped into it (about $28,000 US) and quickly disappeared. And just like that, we owned a piece of Punta Bilar.

Construction has been slow. For the past 18 months, Andot Perlas—a civil engineer married to Ivy's cousin—has periodically sent us the bills. The first few I paid without ceremony or complaint. Then an old pattern kicked in; namely the sensation of actual physical pain upon pressing the "send" button, transferring any significant sum. After a few weeks, I hit on an antidote. "Andote," I said, "never send a bill without including an accompanying photo showing the progress at our house."

The most recent one revealed our shiny new red roof. While those photos have not yet affected a total cure, I can report significant progress. Now, before pressing the send button, I imagine myself sleeping under that roof, having a meal or, my favorite, sharing a drink on the veranda overlooking the vast blue Philippine sea.

It is that vision which sustains me.

8
ROCK STAR

June 14, 2018

Flippant.

That's the best way to describe my usual response when asked why I want to live in the Philippines. My favorite retort: "Because they treat me like a rock star."

I may have to come up with something more imaginative now that it has actually happened.

The occasion was the 2015 publication of my book, "Nazis & Nudists." Basically, it's a memoir, the last third of which recounts the saga of meeting, falling in love with and ultimately marrying the beautiful young Filipina-of-my-dreams with whom I now share life. That portion of the book, of course, takes place mostly amidst the various exotic islands comprising my sweetheart's native land.

Anyone who's ever published a book knows it's not always everything it's cracked up to be. Sure, it's initially ego-gratifying to see your name on the cover of something available on Amazon and, as they say, "wherever good books are sold." (Yeah, I wish.) But then, after the initial flurry of attention from family and friends, you enter the twilight zone of publishing; that amorphous, gray area of unfulfilled fantasies comprising the realization that, despite some attention from the press, a handful of excellent reviews, plus a few of the other kind, no one is actually *buying* the thing. Which results in royalty checks so slim you're embarrassed to show them to your wife, who still thinks you're a big deal.

So it wasn't surprising, when a Filipino journalist friend mentioned the possibility of a book tour in the Philippines, that I jumped at the chance. She quickly put together a modest itinerary consisting mostly of appearances on college campuses, specifically Silliman and Foundation universities in Dumaguete and Surigao State College in the city bearing its name.

There was also, of course, some media involvement, including a feature in the *Sun Star* of Cebu and an appearance on Silliman University TV. But it wasn't until I walked into the first auditorium full of students that the unlikely drama of the situation completely hit home; there, covering nearly the entire wall behind the lectern, hung an enormous poster depicting yours truly holding up the book with his name printed down below. And, most amazingly of all, the place had hardly an empty seat. It didn't hurt, of course, that—as I found out later—the university had made attendance mandatory.

But their response was gratifying; the audience seemed attentive and asked lots of questions. And the pomp was typically Filipino; after each presentation there were proclamations, gifts, plaques, ribbons and, of course, the usual picture-taking sessions. Those took longer than the lectures themselves because, following the formal posing with faculty and administrators, the students literally lined up for selfies.

I had never experienced—nor expected—this kind of treatment. And that's when I realized I was living out my rock star fantasy. So how does a writer, relatively unknown back home, inspire such excitement in the Philippines? The most obvious answer, of course, is that it's a country unaccustomed, at least in the deep provinces, to formal visits from abroad. And that, despite the pronouncements of some politicians and elected officials, most Filipinos still admire Americans.

But there's a larger reason, and it's cultural; the deep-seated Filipino penchant for making strangers feel welcome. That, at its root, is the genesis of their graciousness and the basis of their charm. It's also the thing I like most about this place I find so warm.

9
INSANITY

June 21, 2018

The message was simple, but it took me by surprise. "I love you, Dad. I just called to let you know."

It was my 30-year-old son, Andrew. The last time I'd seen him was a few days earlier at the Alpine Special Treatment Center, a locked residential facility near San Diego, California, that, according to its website, provides "rehabilitative and transitional care to adults suffering from serious mental illness."

It was not unlike the places in which my son has spent much of his adult life and, as happens too often, the visit hadn't been pleasant. Drew–suffering from what professionals call "paranoid schizophrenia"—seemed almost catatonic. While we tried to make conversation, he avoided eye contact, saying little. And as soon as he'd eaten the chicken nuggets we brought as peace offerings, he grunted, "Ok, gotta go now," and disappeared. That was fine with us; at least he hadn't cussed us out and thrown the food in our faces, as had happened on previous occasions.

Such problem are handled differently in the Philippines, a contrast that struck me like a stray bullet during a recent conversation with my wife. Ivy has an aunt, she tells me, who, much like Andrew, has a history of grave mental illness. There are significant differences between the two; my wife's aunt is older, female, and has never shown an inclination towards violence. But there are similarities as well; she admits to hearing voices and has wandered naked on the beach.

And yet, she—unlike my son—has also married and produced several children. And though the family has occasionally consigned her to locked mental health institutions, she has spent most of her life basking in the company of loving relatives and friends.

What is the major difference between the two situations? In a word, it's *family*. Mine in the States, like many there, is emotionally distant and geographically dispersed. And even on the rare occasions that they occupy adjacent spaces, there is little melding of identities of the sort I see regularly among Filipinos.

Ivy's family is more like a tribe; spread far and wide, yet still pervasive in the same island town. When one is broke, the others lend. When one needs help, the others pitch in. And when one is sick, the others take care.

In the auntie's case, the family has housed, fed, and educated her children. They have also taken her in when the need arose. Ivy tells the story of how, when her aunt is feeling desperate and out of control, she sometimes begs relatives to chain her to a tree. And, frequently, Ivy herself has sent funds to provide the vital medications that usually substitute for handcuffs.

The bottom line: back in 1995, when Hillary Clinton published a book called *It Takes a Village,* she could have been talking about the provincial Philippines.

In America, we take solace as we can. A loving phone call from Andrew, we realize, is a small gift often quickly withdrawn. Which is why it didn't surprise me to hear from him again the very next day. "Dad," he said, "I don't want you to visit me anymore. I don't need you, and I don't need your chicken nuggets."

Ahh, but experience tells me his hunger will return.

10
LEFT TURNS

June 28, 2018

It was the announcement you don't want to hear from a pilot. Especially one controlling the airplane on which you're a passenger.

"Attention," said the static-laden voice from the cockpit, "there's good news and bad." The good news, he explained, was that we would eventually reach our destination. The bad: that the airplane couldn't turn right. "Fortunately," the cheeky pilot concluded, "there are no right turns en route to Manila."

As we rumbled toward takeoff from Surigao Airport, I couldn't help but think of a moth circling left over a drain.

We have an expression in America about highly resourceful people using "chewing gum" to fix things when nothing else is available. I can't quite recall the first time I realized how handy Filipinos are with chewing gum; perhaps several years ago when my Filipino father-in-law first came to live with us in Southern California.

He doesn't speak much English. We quickly learned to communicate, though, when I saw him dragging an enormous TV set in a little red wagon across my front lawn. He'd been down the road for the weekly outdoor flea market and seen an offer he couldn't refuse.

Let me say at the outset that I'm not opposed to television. Truth be told, I've spent more than a few happy hours gazing at a set or two myself. This one, however, differed significantly from the ones to which I'm accustomed; for starters, it was almost the size of a Volkswagen Beetle and probably just as old. On top of it sat a flimsy-looking set of rabbit ears, the kind I hadn't seen in years. And when we turned the thing on, well, the picture wasn't much better than if we'd left it unplugged.

But taped to that pitch-black screen was a tiny white sign. "FREE," it said, written in what appeared to be the shaky hand of someone cleaning house. For my father-in-law, it was a deal made in heaven.

"But it's a piece of junk," I objected. "Why should we be storing other people's junk?"

"I can fix," he insisted.

So now we have a working TV set installed under the patio awning of our California house. There are other examples of such thriftiness involving my father-in-law and his ilk. One caused a huge argument about moving from the city to the desert.

It had to do with a set of ancient bar stools with badly rotted seats. For me, the solution was simple; throw them away and buy a new pair. But he had a different idea, insisting that we take them with us to our new house. He also persuaded me, against my better judgment, to keep a smelly backyard woodpile I hadn't noticed in years. The upshot? Bar stools, naturally, with nicely fitted wooden seats adorning the spaces around our Jacuzzi.

Believe me, I get it. The Philippines is steeped in poverty. Because new goods are scarce, Filipinos make do with what they have by figuring out ingenious, if sometimes tedious, ways of using things forever. The cardinal rule among provincials: never, under any circumstances, throw anything away.

Which brings us back to that airplane in Surigao. The initial announcement came after an hour of sitting on the tarmac; airport officials had delayed our takeoff, they said, because of a "problem with the controls." But they hadn't canceled the flight, an attendant assured us; kindly return to the terminal until mechanics can correct the problem.

Two hours later, they ushered us back aboard with the somewhat startling news that the airplane could only turn left. And so we flew to Manila without a single right turn. All of which left me both impressed and utterly terrified. The only significant unanswered question: exactly what brand of chewing gum did those resourceful mechanics use?

11
THE TROUBLE WITH TIME

May 24, 2018

For a long time, it seemed like forever. Then, suddenly, forever arrived.

It was a decade ago that we thought of moving to the Philippines. One day, after twenty-three years as a *Los Angeles Times* staff writer, I arrived at work to hear my boss say, "Let's take a walk." It was a long one, down a corridor traversed many times en route to the company cafeteria. This time, however, the destination was different; the Human Resources Department, a fact that dawned on me only gradually as that infamous office began drawing near.

"You know these are hard times for newspapers," my boss began, "and today is especially hard for the *Times*."

That's when it hit me like a punch in the gut. What he was saying, I suddenly realized, was that it would be an especially hard day for *me*. Plus a few dozen others who, by its end, would be unemployed.

It was several hours before I had the courage to tell my wife. By then she had been in the US just under five months, and our marriage had barely begun. How do you tell someone who's left everything behind for a new life abroad that the new life is now uncertain? More to the point, how do you tell yourself? Who was I now that I was no longer who I was?

It was only after staring into the abyss of those eternal questions that our new idea was born; why not, we fantasized, chuck it all and start anew? And why not do it in the land of Ivy's birth?

Thinking of something and making it real, of course, are two different things. God knows I'd already spent enough time in the Philippines by then to know that I liked it. But visiting differs from staying. Both of us realized it would require a great deal of planning to make our dream come true.

And so we began.

Eventually I got a new job, though not as good as the old. Ivy, too, who had earned a degree in medical technology in the Philippines, went to work as soon as she could. And then, in what I can only describe as traditional American fashion, she toiled, studied, and clawed her way forward until a fairly good job became an outstanding career.

I went the other way. My career had already peaked, so when our son was born in 2010, I started winding down. I announced my retirement to become a stay-at-home-dad. Then, a few years later, signed up for social security and started drawing my pension.

It was around this time that forever began. We sold our house in Long Beach, California, bought a cheaper one in a less-expensive part of the state and used the equity to build our new home abroad. And while Ivy concentrated on earning as much as she could, I held down the home front and prepared for our intercontinental move. Though we still had lots to do, it seemed like we had forever to do it. Then the end of forever slid alarmingly close.

We are now eight weeks from moving day and suddenly I'm in a panic. To be sure, keeping our California house will make things easier. We won't, for instance, be disposing of any furniture or making painful decisions regarding what not to keep. Nor will enormous shipping bills smother us to death.

Still, there are many things to do. In the next two months, we must re-organize our finances, dispose of our car, teach someone to service the backyard hot tub and, well, pack for the rest of our lives. Not to mention, of course, get our documents in order and bid farewell to our friends. When I lay it all out, it doesn't seem like much. And yet, I'm enveloped in dread.

For what is approaching is a kind of death; the demise of an old life and the birth of a new one. Like any reincarnation, it is both scary and exciting. Above all, though, it is *real* because the time has grown so short.

That's the trouble with time. It sneaks up on you, stealthily, like a snake. And if you're not careful, it will bite you in the behind.

12
A KIND OF DEATH

July 26, 2018

It feels like a kind of death. Everywhere I go, I wonder whether it's the last time I'll ever be there. Each thing I do seems like something I may never do again. A friend recently wondered whether I realized that this could be my "last and final move." Another spoke somewhat more directly: "Do you think you'll die there?" she soberly asked.

What they're referring to is our imminent move to the Philippines. By the time you read this, our life here will be over and the first throes of a new one begun.

For now, though, I am focused more on what I'm leaving behind than on any promise the future may hold. For a cloud shrouds the future in fog, while the past is clear and bright.

We've had a good life in the US. Both of us have engaged in meaningful work. The community to which we moved three years ago has embraced us with open hearts. And what once was an empty house in the California desert has become a much-loved home.

So why are we doing this, anyway? We conceived the plan to move to Ivy's home province of Surigao del Norte several years ago. Our world was quite different back then, as I have explained. I had tumbled from a beloved career position into a job I hated and toiled at for half the pay. Ivy's career as a medical lab scientist had not yet blossomed. And living in coastal Southern California had become more expensive than we could afford.

So, leaning toward the country of her origin, we hatched a plan of escape. First, we bought some land there and started building a house. Then, to minimize the burning of bridges, we moved to a small town called Joshua Tree in the California desert, where life is a lot cheaper. So cheap, in fact, that—aided by rental income—we fully expect to keep our little desert abode even when we are no longer its primary inhabitants.

As I've said before, it was an exceedingly long-range plan. But even long ranges eventually end, and we have finally come to the end of ours. Both of us have given notice at our jobs. I've gotten a 13A permanent residency visa and purchased airline tickets. We have packed what we think we can carry and are sending the rest ahead. And soon we will host a farewell party to bid adieu to our friends.

All of which should be extremely exciting, of course, but here's the thing; the tickets are one-way. And so, between bouts of excitement, I am experiencing the pangs of loss. Sometimes they are pervasive enough to tug at my heart and moisten my eyes. At other times, I'm sure they make me irritable and difficult to live with for the people I love.

There's only one antidote, and that is time. Enough of it must pass so that I am more involved in the future's rebirth than the death of the past, more focused on what's ahead than on what is behind, and too busy creating a new life to mourn the passing of the old.

I pray and expect it will all happen soon.

13
HOME

Aug. 2, 2018

The thing that finally got to me was the abundance of tears. Some belonged to friends plainly sad to see us go. When even my ex-wife joined the chorus of grief, however, I knew that the turning point we'd reached was not ours alone.

"I thought I could get through this without breaking down," sobbed the woman with whom I'd shared fifteen years and conceived two children over three decades before. Both of us had remarried and long since recovered from the ancient pain we'd inflicted on each other. In fact, my former wife had grown so fond of my new Filipino one that she'd consented to become the godmother of our only son. "I'm going to miss both of you," she choked now, hugging Ivy and me tightly to her chest. "Please don't forget me."

The scene had taken place in the waning moments of the farewell party we'd thrown for relatives and friends before embarking from the California desert to the jungles of the Philippines. Lots of excellent food, alcoholically enhanced laughter, and, frankly, bad karaoke, had marked the gathering. But then came those last few moments when our guests began saying their goodbyes with that unanswerable question hovering over their heads like so many comic book speech bubbles; would they ever see us again?

The question was on our minds too, as we arose early the next morning for the long ride to the airport. There followed, of course, the usual travails of traveling; growling stomachs combined with aching rear ends, cramped movies with barely audible sound, and sleep patterns completely torn to shreds.

By the time we arrived for our five-hour layover in Shanghai, China, we felt ready for anything. Not, however, for the humorless treatment received at the hands of unsmiling airport personnel barking orders as if dealing with cattle. Not for the stern security officer who ran my carry-on through the x-ray machine three times before ripping open a newly purchased shaving kit to discard a pair of scissors just a fraction too big. And not for the sour food server who looked like she'd rather be anywhere but there.

Ah, but then we landed in Cebu, the second largest city in the Philippines, and suddenly the atmosphere changed. By then it was 3 a.m., yet everyone seemed happy to see us. A fetchingly friendly female immigration officer cracked open the sealed envelope containing my resident visa, welcomed us with a smile and suggested that I report to the immigration office in Surigao City–our ultimate destination–within seven days to pick up my Alien Certificate of Registration card. And when we went to the transfer desk to catch our domestic flight out, several staffers collaborated to minimize the extra-luggage charge. That's when a familiar feeling came over me, the sense of relief, happiness, and lightheartedness I'd experienced before. It was as if a great weight had been lifted and I was back in the place I knew and loved.

It hasn't all been smooth sailing since, to be sure. It turns out that the fetchingly friendly female immigration officer was dead wrong; to get my ACR card, I must return to Cebu. So, after a great deal of emergency re-scheduling, we have made plans to do just that. And because we have not yet finished our new home, we expect to spend the next several weeks living out of suitcases in a series of exceedingly small rooms.

Two days ago, though, we caught the ferry to Siargao Island. There, outside a rustic beach resort near General Luna, I spent an hour lying in a hammock over steaming white sand shared only by a sleeping dog. And in the morning, the voice of a young child singing next door awakened us early amidst a cacophony of crowing roosters.

That's when I knew I was home.

14
MAKING IT REAL

Aug. 10, 2018

It was as if my entire life hung on the strength of a flickering internet signal. Another minute of darkness, it seemed, and this wonderful new world would be gone.

Let me begin by saying that I've never harbored much sympathy for illegal immigrants in the United States. I've always figured if my wife and half her family can do it legally, well, so can anyone else. I might have to soften my stance, however, based on my first week as a new immigrant to the Philippines. I still don't favor illegals. But part of me, I must admit, bears some newfound empathy where previously there was none.

The immigration woes that brought me to this radical new understanding started, quite unbeknownst to me, in the guise of that aforementioned officer in Cebu. "Of course," she smilingly assured me, "just go to the Surigao immigration office within seven days to process your visa."

The visa to which she referred was the permanent residency (13A) for which I had painstakingly applied at the Philippine Consulate in Los Angeles. It had taken some doing, to be sure, but not nearly as much, one consular official assured me, as his counterparts in the Philippines would require. After submitting the paperwork–including police and medical clearances, financial disclosures, a letter from Ivy requesting my residency and a cashier's check for $150 US–everything was ready to pick up in just over a week. Specifically, *everything* consisted of a passport sticker allowing me to enter the county on a one-way ticket and a sealed envelope immigration officials would open at our port of entry.

That official turned out to be the Cebuana, who confidently waved us toward our ultimate destination. From where, secure in knowing I had plenty of time, we embarked on the long recreational weekend on Siargao Island before getting down to the serious business at hand.

Imagine my surprise a few days later when the fine folks at Immigration Surigao informed me that, no, they had no means of processing my application; what I had to do was return to Cebu.

And so up went the first of many red flags. Quickly re-arranging our plans, we hopped aboard the next overnight ferry for the 10-hour trip to the city in question. Which would get us, by my reckoning, at the immigration office in Cebu on day six of the allotted seven..

That's when the internet failed.

Trust me, it had been working fine earlier that morning when we first arrived. But then they sent us off to another office across town called the Bureau of Quarantine, where I got tested for syphilis, had my picture taken and underwent a brief interview by the presiding physician. Fortunately, no venereal diseases were found (whew!), so we took a fast cab back to the immigration department. Only to learn that the all-important Manila internet connection had fallen down and couldn't get back up.

"Something having to do with Globe," an official-looking official earnestly explained, mentioning one of the country's leading internet providers. "It might come back up this afternoon, or maybe tomorrow."

When they hadn't restored the signal by 3 p.m., we knew we had arrived at a crossroads. So, Ivy caught the next ferry back to Surigao, while I rented a room in Cebu.

And that's when I had my great epiphany; the outcome, I realized, was completely out of my hands. The internet connection would come up–or not–and I would meet the seven-day deadline, or I wouldn't. And that this was the reality with which I would have to make peace to survive in this great unwashed nation of islands. There was also a corollary: that making peace with uncertainty might just make me a better man.

The next morning, I dutifully returned to the immigration office where, praise Jesus, the internet connection had also returned! Of course, I wasn't yet out of the woods; there were still lines to fall into, documents to copy, pictures to take, fingerprints to grab and the minor matter of another 6,447 pesos ($121 US) to pay.

So when would the coveted Alien Certificate of Registration card finally be mine? "Oh," an official casually informed me, "don't worry; it will be here in two or three months." And how would they inform me? "We won't," he said without hesitation, "just come back to see if it's ready."

I pray the ferries run on time.

15
SQUATTING ROCK

Aug. 16, 2018

The smile on the old woman's face said it all. It bore creases, like twisted canyons burned into a hard-brown mountain in the shapes of scars. Senona Espiel was a 92-year-old unmarried woman who'd never had a birthday party. By the end of the day, she'd just be a 92-year-old unmarried woman.

My wife, Ivy, had planted the seed of this change a week earlier when she and her great-great aunt discovered they shared more than just blood. The old woman had come into the world on August 3rd, 1926, while Ivy showed up on the same day just 56 years later. And so, we planned a joint birthday party at Magpupungko Beach, where the old woman had spent her whole life.

The name means "squatting rock" after an enormous boulder balancing precariously over the pristine tide pools as if it's about to fall, a metaphor perhaps for the fragility of life in these parts. It is here on Siargao Island that generations of my wife's family lived and died, argued, struggled, gave birth, and, sometimes, lay intoxicated under the coconut trees. In 2006, when I first saw it, Magpupungko was a stretch of virgin white sand, the most beautiful place I'd ever seen. A year later, we built the first structure there, a tiny thatched-roof cottage with a ragged heart cut into its ceiling as a token of our love. Today, the beach is hardly recognizable, with a concrete barrier dividing the sand from the coconuts and restrooms, as well as a myriad of refreshment stands everywhere. And local officials have constructed a gate where they collect 50 pesos per head (about $1 US) from busloads of entering tourists. Ivy owns a large piece of it—inherited from her father, who inherited it from his–and her cousin owns an even larger parcel on the other side. It is there that Ivy's great, great aunt Senona–affectionately called *Uya Noning,* an honorific title meaning "great grandmother"—was born and still lives.

She doesn't know exactly how long her family has been here; probably, she believes, since the era of Spanish colonial rule. After over nine decades, her memories have faded, but one remains clear; the time her father ordered her to hide in the jungle from the Japanese soldiers who had landed on the beach. They were there for the *tuba*; the sweet intoxicating nectar made from the sap of coconut trees. As they gathered the translucent liquid in their makeshift jugs, the young girl watched warily from the branches above their heads, finally climbing down only in the evening after the soldiers had taken their leave. Years later, she got engaged to a man who loved her, but he grew sick and died before they could perform the nuptials to consummate their union. And so, *Uya Noning* passed her years quietly here on the beach called Squatting Rock.

The party started early with a traditional rendition of "Happy Birthday" sung over a cake adorned by two flickering candles. The elderly woman needed help in blowing them out, so Ivy obliged with some breath of her own. Then the tributes began from the dozens of relatives on hand for this most special of occasions. When it was all over, the old lady sat beaming in a way seldom seen, her face marked by a smile transcending what had looked like a scar.

"My heart is bursting," she whispered in her native *Bisaya* as Ivy wiped away the old woman's tears.

Much later, long after the tourists had departed and the honored auntie gone to bed, the clan claiming both her and my beloved wife danced wildly on the beach, drinking bottles of Red Horse, and holding their children's hands. And that's when I realized how lucky I was to find them, how honored to be included in this most amazing night under the giant rock squatting over the sand.

16
THE CHAOS OF CHANGE

Aug. 23, 2018

The most disconcerting thing about it is that it's never constant. It shows up at the most inopportune times, buzzing in your ear like an annoying fly, then recedes, leaving a strong sense of thankfulness and relief even in the wake of its imminent return.

Chaos.

I have spent a lifetime battling it, avoiding it, creating a space in which it cannot and does not thrive. Yet, here it is—an old foe from long ago—once again popping up to say hello.

Including travel time, we are now entering week four of our new life in the Philippines. Though our seaside house is far from complete, the engineer promises one small bedroom and bathroom ready this week, so we have someplace to stay.

In the meantime, we are hanging out at a modest pension house for 700 pesos per night, around $12 US. It's not bad; there's air conditioning, a flushing toilet, and a shower that even gets hot. There's a parking space in back for our car. And yet there's something else here as well; the feeling that chaos is knocking at our door.

As I say, it's not always there. Everything seems perfectly in order and exactly as it should be. Then something trips a hidden wire, and the beast within us roars. It's usually something trivial; we have no internet or forget to buy water and realize we won't have breakfast in the morning. We get lost on the way home, driving recklessly through the streets. Or, most often and with maximum effect, something we know we brought with us just disappears; my slippers, for instance, or the shaver that perfectly contours my face.

That's when the imagination goes into overdrive. What on God's earth are we doing here? What the hell were we thinking?

For Ivy, the feeling of encroaching chaos seems more tied up with work. It is she who gave up a blossoming and lucrative career in medical science to return to the place of her birth. The discovery that she would have to go back to school to resume that career here has sent her into an emotional tailspin.

For me, it's more existential. I too, of course, am bothered by the sparse quarters and paucity of order. But they are ripples on the surface of a deeper lagoon. At the heart of that dark body of water, trapped in the purple rocks that form its core, is the primordial ooze over which most of us spend our lives constructing bridges. It is the darkness of disorientation, the ooze of nothingness, the black hole of emptiness in which we fear getting lost. To prevent that from happening, we cover that jagged precipice with jobs, schedules, relationships, obligations, familiar surroundings, friends, and, yes, beautifully constructed homes.

Moving to a foreign country rips all that away. And so, feeling the encroaching chaos, I think of the sunny, many-windowed house in which we one day shall live, and the darkness quickly recedes. I read an essay once describing humans as time travelers who transcend barriers between present and future by envisioning the future to make it real in the now. Perhaps that's the bridge that gets us across. I pray it won't, to borrow the title of an American movie classic, be a bridge too far.

17
WINDOW

Aug. 30, 2018

It's kind of like a window we've been aiming at for years and finally passed through. Yesterday Ivy brought cotton, fruit, water, and rice to the big house for good luck. Then she spent hours arranging furniture and sharing intimacies with a broom. Finally, last night we ate *lechon*, a traditional roasted pig dish, in the garage with a coterie of workers, relatives, well-wishers, and friends before retiring to our untested beds. And this morning I write my first words from our new home in Punta Bilar.

The house is far from finished. There are loose wires everywhere, piles of wet cement, floors that need tiling and walls that need painting. But two small bedrooms and a restroom on the bottom floor are more-or-less complete. So, we have claimed them as our own, while, above and around us, the directed chaos of construction continues.

The tiny organic accouterments placed in a strategically located bowl, Ivy tells me, are to make our existence here respectively soft, abundant, and sweet. The purpose of the *lechon* is more obvious; to celebrate the beginnings of a new life in a vastly different place.

Last night's party was sweet. People with paper plates lined up at makeshift tables, laughing as the hot evening wind blew in from the sea. It felt like the ocean was breathing on them, smiling kindly on the minor efforts of these awestruck humans at its side. Elsewhere and higher up, visitors toured the house, taking care not to step in its cracks. And as I sat on the upstairs veranda drinking *Tanduay*—an island rum highly popular in the Philippines—while staring into the gaping abyss below, it occurred to me that I had arrived.

I recall a time long ago in my early twenties when I spent a summer camping out on the pristine beach of a Greek island with a bunch of naked hippies. An older man lived there, an American who had a big house overlooking the Mediterranean Sea. One night he invited us up for dinner, and I remember wondering how he had created a life like this; how had he gotten to this stunning place of awe?

Now I am him.

I don't know how these things happen. I don't know why one person ends up starving to death while another no more deserving spends his later years living in a big house overlooking Surigao Strait. Perhaps such things are not for us to know, but simply enjoy, be grateful for, and share.

We hope this gathering will not be the last in this big, bright house by the sea. We hope our new home will be a place of joy and comfort, not only for us but for all those who visit. God knows, we have a great deal to do; for a while we will fall asleep to the smell of sawdust and awaken to the sound of hammers.

We will solve these problems in time. Meanwhile, I woke up this morning to breakfast on a veranda next to a lighthouse with the sound of the Eagles' "Hotel California" tickling my pink ears more loudly than the carpenters' pounds. And I knew then, as I did the first time I came here and many times since, that this is exactly the place I belong.

18
BROWNOUT

Sept. 6, 2018

It always happens at the most inopportune time. You're having dinner with friends about to make a point that, you're convinced, will finally identify you as the genius you know yourself to be. Or, better, you're sitting on the potty reading the Sunday paper just about to flush. When suddenly the lights go off.

It would be bad enough simply having to carry on in total darkness sans air conditioning. In our case, though, the high elevation requires the pumping of water up from an underground vault below. That pump is electric. Thus, when the lights go out so does showering, shaving, and flushing. When power outages happen here, to put it another way, one's continued survival becomes an exercise in primitive living.

We have always recognized, of course, that this sort of thing happens often in the Philippines. That's why we designed our house to include a diesel-operated generator providing power in precisely such situations. But the generator has yet to arrive.

And so, God–who clearly has a well-developed sense of humor–gave us a little gift to welcome us to our new home; not one, but *two*, major brownouts in as many days. I can sum up my immediate reaction to those twenty-some hours of insufferable heat, impenetrable darkness, stagnant water, and stinking toilets roughly this way: what the hell am I doing here? Or, more succinctly; whatever was I thinking, please take me home now.

Nobody took me home, of course. Instead, Ivy and I–along with our seven-year-old son, Isaac–soldiered through those two grueling nights.

Rather than expressing my doubts, I swallowed them, and I'm sure my wife did the same. And then a miracle happened; God said, "let there be electricity" and suddenly there was.

It took a few days, though, to fully absorb what had happened. That crack in consciousness occurred during a late-night tour of our three-story house. During the day, while workers pound nails and exercise saws on the upper floors, we confine ourselves to the basement. On this night, though, I expanded my horizons by venturing upwards after dark. And what I saw completely changed my perspective on our own petty suffering.

In a word, it was a cadre of construction workers sleeping on wooden pallets. Six of them. Scattered at various points on the dusty debris-splattered floor. Without air conditioning, lights, or even mattresses.

I knew, of course, that some workers were spending their nights at our construction-site-of-a-house rather than returning home to their families. I'd also been told that they bathed in a nearby stream and relieved themselves God knows where. But I had never actually seen them.

And seeing them now had a definite effect. Specifically, it reminded me that our standard of living–even without electricity, air conditioning, running water or flushing toilets–is still better than that of many Filipinos. And it made me ashamed of having been such a crybaby.

In the end, I realized that what I thought had been God's joke was really his lesson, and it was this; that my family and I are privileged. And privilege is something one should never take for granted or forget.

19
DISCONNECTED

Sept. 13, 2018

It started as a tiny niggle. The pocket Wi-Fi we'd purchased just wasn't putting out the way it should. Then we noticed our cell phones weren't connecting. And finally came some devastating news; neither Globe nor Smart–the two major internet providers in the Philippines–would service our neighborhood because, well, there just weren't enough customers to make it pay.

Suddenly the niggle became a major toothache. In fact, it was a deep and unrelenting source of existential angst. No internet? That would keep us completely disconnected. Without a signal, how would we survive?

I count myself among the rapidly shrinking number of human beings old enough to remember life before the internet, a time when people communicated by calling each other on telephones connected to actual wires, sending letters through the postal service or—just imagine—talking face-to-face!

Wait, let me rephrase that; I don't *remember* that time, I know I was there because I've seen pictures of myself allegedly taking part in it. And, of course, I've also heard stories about how people--apparently including me–somehow conducted their lives without even a small piece of cyberspace to call their own.

In fact, I remember the first time I ever heard of email. It was in the old newsroom of the *Los Angeles Times*; one day, a fellow reporter beckoned me and several others to her desk. "Check this out," she said, clearly excited. "You type a message to someone, and they can see it on their computer!" We all stood around watching in awe as she showed us how this newfangled gimmick worked. Wow, very cool, we agreed, but what practical purpose would it ever serve?

While I retain vague visual and auditory impressions of the pre-internet world, I have no inkling of how it felt to live in it. Frankly, it's as if I was never really there. And now, God forbid, I face the prospect of not being anywhere at all.

We haven't yet fully surrendered to the inevitability of traveling backwards in time. We still have a few tricks up our collective sleeve. After speaking with the representatives of Globe and Smart, we visited the offices of another company called PLDT. Yes, they told us; they do indeed offer Internet service in Punta Bilar, but only for businesses holding valid Mayor's permits. But, *wink wink*, the sales agent said, "let me see what I can do."

We are still awaiting his call.

Then, just yesterday, a friend gave us a router attached to a powerful and exceptionally large antenna. If we can put the antenna high enough, he claims, it will pick up a signal from town. Tomorrow we plan to install the damn thing as high on our roof as we can.

In the meantime, there are some short-term fixes. Ivy's sister, who lives in the city, gets a good signal at her house, though not the best I've ever seen. A few days ago, we called Globe to boost her service at our expense. And we've discovered a coffee shop at the mall downtown offering Wi-Fi that's not too bad.

Suddenly we're drinking lots of coffee.

20
PARADE

Sept. 20, 2018
I have always loved parades. Only one, however, made me cry. I'm speaking of the 34th annual *Bonok-Bonok* street dancing spectacle held last week in Surigao City.

The disclosure that it brought tears to my eyes, frankly, is a bit embarrassing. I'm supposed to be the cynical, hard-bitten former newspaper reporter who's seen and heard it all. No maudlin sentimentality here! And yet, as I watched the city's finest youngsters dance their hearts out bathed in colorful costumes from somewhere east of Wonderland, well, it spoke to me in a way few events ever have.

Bonok-Bonok is the town's annual fiesta honoring its patron saint, San Nicolas de Tolentino. Anyone who's ever been to the Philippines will tell you that every city, town, and barangay holds a fiesta each year honoring the saint for which its founding fathers felt a particular affinity. There are so many, in fact, that wherever you are in the country, it's a safe bet that at least one fiesta is raging somewhere nearby. And, for many Filipinos, the local fiesta is the most joyful time of the year next to Christmas.

In Surigao, *Banok-Banok* refers to a traditional dance of the native *Mamanwa* tribe thanking the gods for abundance. It features the celebrated street-dance parade followed by an extravagant ethnic dance show in the provincial sports complex and, of course, the usual *lechon* feasts citywide. In fact, I'd seen it before. Several years ago, when Ivy and I were still living in California with only vague notions of moving to Surigao, we visited the city during its fiesta. Though I'd enjoyed the parade immensely, another considerably less pleasant experience marred its memory; getting trapped in an overcrowded stadium by security guards who, for reasons unfathomable then and now, simply refused to let us go.

This time we skipped the big dance show, contenting ourselves with just the parade. And as the first group made its way down the street with drums banging out a loud cadence and school-age children moving in unified splendor, well, a strange chill took hold.

I think it had to do with the intensity. *"Viva Surigao, maradjao, karadjao!"* the dancing young people chanted, their faces glowing in pleasure with lips streaked by smiles. "Viva Surigao; outstandingly excellent!" And it struck me that I hadn't seen this kind of ferocious glee for one's hometown in ages, certainly not among children and never about anything except a winning sports team.

Anyone who's ever practiced journalism will tell you it invades your blood and stays there long after you have taken your leave for saner pursuits. And so, without even thinking, I stood directly in the parade's path with a line of actual credentialed journalists snapping pictures as the adrenalin pulsed. That's when I felt the telltale drop in my eye; An unstoppable surge of excitement sparked, yes, by being part of the action again but, more than that, by the sheer expressions of joy on the faces of those blessed children.

Several times, security guards had to shove my comrades and me to the sidelines to make way for the parade. Later, a reporter for the local radio station grabbed me for a live man-on-the-street interview regarding my reactions to the day's events. "Spectacular!" I breathed into his proffered microphone. "Splendid! I love the fervor; it lifts my soul. *Viva Surigao, maradjao, karadjao!"*

Just another day, I reflected, in my new hometown.

21
DAVID SALAD

Oct. 4, 2018

As some are wont to do, I have occasionally entertained fantasies of fame. What I never imagined, though, was achieving it as a salad. And yet, at a certain restaurant in Surigao City, there it is in big flashy letters on the menu: "SPECIAL OF THE MONTH; DAVID SALAD, 200 pesos."

Oh fame, delicious fame.

It came about as a complete surprise. One day I walked into a place called Andreani's on Surigao's main tourist drag, known locally as "The Boulevard," because, well, I'd never seen it before. I was kind of hungry, but not enough to allow the restaurant's menu to enslave me.

"I don't see any salads," I complained to the server after perusing her offerings. Turns out she wasn't just a server, but the owner.

"We can make you one," she quickly assured me. "What would you like us to put in it?"

"Hm, lettuce," I said. "And how about some carrots?"

"Sure," she said easily. "Fish?"

"No."

"Meat?"

"No."

"Fruits?"

"Sounds good," I said.

She promptly marched into the kitchen and began barking orders in *Surigaonon*. And almost immediately, I could hear earnest chopping, probably on a wooden block.

While the two of us waited for the chef's ingenuity to present itself for our inspection, we had a pleasant chat. Her name was Ellen Bonilla Schmid, she informed me, a native of Surigao, now married to a Swiss national with whom she lives in Singapore. But they owned property in the Philippines too, including this restaurant which had opened a few months before. And so far, she said, business had been just so-so. One of the major challenges; how to attract the many foreigners who frequented this part of town.

"Well, this foreigner likes salad," I offered and, as if on cue, up walked a young girl–the *real* server–toting a salad the likes of which I had never seen. Not only did it have lettuce and carrots without meat or seafood; it also sported fresh cucumbers, hard-boiled eggs, onions, sliced mangos, and shredded coconut. Not to mention, a lovely green mustard dressing that beckoned my tongue like a siren beckoning a sailor. And here's the topper; they served it with a fork instead of the usual Philippine spoon.

"Wow, this looks great!" I stammered, digging in. Bottom line: the chef's ingenuity did not disappoint. "You should put it on your menu," I joked. "You could call it David's Salad."

OK, fast forward a week; I walk in, and there it is. "We've had so many requests," explains Bernadette, Ellen's sister, "that we made it this month's special." Then she introduces me to some other cast members: sister number two, Catherine; niece Angelica, the server; chef James, a cousin, and official David Salad chopper, Gemuel Cagasan. "Mostly foreigners order it," Bernadette continues. "They all ask who David is."

Take a guess at what I ordered for dinner.

Being known as a salad is heady stuff, of course, but there's also a deeper message. First, given the proper incentive, Filipinos can fix, create, put together, cook, or eat anything with whatever materials they have on hand. Second, theirs is a land, at least for me, where wonderful fantasies come true. And, finally, if you're ever in Surigao City, check out Andreani's on The Boulevard, just up from the Tavern Hotel.

The place serves an outstanding salad.

22
STUCK!

Oct. 11, 2018

It was the thud that breaks your heart. The kind that gives you a sinking feeling, both literally and figuratively. The kind that says, in menacing terms; ok, bud, you're stuck! Now let's see if you can get yourself free...

My gut told me loudly that I couldn't.

We had set out earlier that day in our 2011 Toyota Fortuner to see a surveyor in a distant barangay. To get there, we had taken a circuitous route along highways fronting the ocean and busy passages through cluttered streets. Now we had turned onto a very narrow street with huge clumps of its pavement missing on one side. To avoid the resulting potholes, you had to navigate to the left between them while the oncoming traffic–quite considerable given the road's condition–waited for you to pass. Then quickly return to your rightful lane to let the accumulated cars and their patient drivers flow by.

"Wow, this is insane," I remarked to my wife's young nephew, who, thankfully, had offered to drive.

That's when we heard the thud. Not loud, mind you, but soft, almost gentle, as if not wishing to offend. Followed by a sickening jerk as the car suddenly halted, careening wildly to one side. It wasn't difficult to glean what had happened; in avoiding the huge potholes, we had eased too far left, forcing our front tire into an unmarked gully traversing that side of the road. Now it was stuck there, buried to its hubcaps in mud.

Hoping against all hope, I commandeered the driver's seat, threw the gearshift into reverse, and stepped hard on the gas. Only to hear the back tire spinning fruitlessly against the pavement as the smell of burning rubber permeated the air. Yup, I uttered to myself in disgust, we're definitely stuck. "Damn!" There seemed to be no escape.

Anyone who's seen a Fortuner knows it's no compact car. In the USA, my next move would be to call the auto club for roadside assistance. Or, more likely, someone would already be summoning police to report the unacceptable blockage of traffic. But this was the provincial Philippines. And so a young Filipino man, perhaps the driver of a vehicle inconvenienced by our dilemma, stepped up to help.

He was but the first. Over the next several minutes, they kept coming, seemingly out of nowhere, materializing as if saintly spirits charged with our protection. Until there were, I swear, fifteen men. Without a word, they organized themselves into teams. One man took the wheel, another jacked up the disobedient tire with a stick and stones gathered from the roadside, while the rest formed a muscled squad of pushers to force the car from its trap. One heave-ho, and the deed was done. Then, just as quickly as they had appeared, our army of saviors vanished into the undulating afternoon without a trace, leaving before we could say thank you or goodbye.

So what has this experience taught?

First, there are roads in the Philippines worse than most Western countries would allow. More significantly, though, I have witnessed firsthand a perfect example of Filipino self-reliance, teamwork, and community spirit. It is necessary. It is pervasive. And, unlike certain other aspects of this culture, it is decisive.

Bottom line: you could do far worse in life than getting stuck in the Philippines.

23
AMOEBA

Oct. 18, 2018

I don't know what it is about me and salads. Two weeks ago, I had one named after me. And this week a different one put me in the hospital. Perhaps sharing your name with a salad is akin to marriage; being unfaithful is more than unwise.

My own near-fatal infidelity began as many do; with what seemed like an innocent flirtation. We had spent the morning at the local mall, picking up some things we needed. By the time we finished it was lunchtime, so I suggested eating at a restaurant we had never tried. And there it was, staring seductively up at me from the menu; the sweetest, most demure, delicious-looking little salad I had ever seen.

"I'll take that," I said to the waitress, pointing to my new heartthrob's picture. And I swear, it was as if the salad winked at me; I should have known then that I was deeply in trouble.

We had our first spat just hours later when I felt a twitching in my stomach. It was as if someone trapped in there desperately wanted out. The massive getaway that followed was utter and complete; a dramatic escape from both exits without a moment's hesitation or doubt.

And that describes my next several days.

Here's the thing about Philippine hospitals; you got your public and your private. My wife, who works in the medical field, says while the level of care at the city's large public hospital is quite good, its waiting rooms stay crowded with lines very long.

I was clearly in no shape to wait.

So we made our way to the emergency room of the privately owned Surigao Medical Center. And, sure enough, within an hour they had admitted me to the hospital for treatment of yup, one particularly nasty little intestinal amoeba. My private room was not luxurious, though it included all the basics; adjustable bed, bathroom, air conditioning, cable TV and a small extra bed for a "watcher" of my choosing. My loving wife initially filled that position, doing an incredible job of tending to my every need. This being the Philippines, of course, various other family members also got involved; at one point, in fact, three people shared that tiny single bed.

Life in a Philippine hospital is nothing if not charming. One of the most charming moments came around 5 a.m. each morning when a doe-eyed Filipino nurse would waltz in, flip on the lights, and cheerfully ask about the size, frequency, color, texture, and consistency of my previous night's bowel movements. Another charming moment... oh, never mind, I think you get the point.

After three days and nights, endless interrogations, lots of medications and the expert tutelage of the excellent Dr. Francis Mantilla, I got to go home. The final price tag: 26,336.84 pesos, the equivalent of about $485 US. Around what it would cost under Medicare back home.

So what have I learned from this lovely—and, one might add, explosive—experience? Mainly to never cheat on a salad. No, from this day forward, it's just me and that special one until death do us part. Which, based on my experience so far, could be sooner rather than later.

24
WATCHING THE PAINT DRY

Oct. 25, 2018

It's not as if we have nothing else to do. There's cooking, washing clothes, taking Isaac to school, shopping and, of course, visiting friends. Lately, though, we've been using what little spare time we do have in a novel way. I call it watching the paint dry.

If you're wondering what paint looks like drying, well, you're right to wonder. It doesn't look like anything. And that's the point; as we sit in the basement ostensibly watching our new house growing up around us, we sometimes feel as if we're living in a state of suspended animation. Nothing moves. Nothing changes for days, even weeks. Sometimes we suspect the paint has already dried, and we just don't know it.

Several weeks ago, we had what we hoped would be an enlightening meeting with our engineer who, I hasten to add, we hold in high regard. "Friend," we told him, as gently as we could, "it seems like we'll be living in the basement with the ants for years. We don't want to spend even *one* year living with the ants; Is there anything you can do?"

He nodded earnestly in understanding and immediately went off to confer with the foreman. And for a while, the pace picked up and we noticed some improvement.

Then I spent three days in the hospital describing my poop to beautiful Filipino nurses, followed by an immediate week-long sojourn to Siargao Island for General Luna's fiesta. On the boat ride home, we fantasized about what we would find. "Maybe they've finished the house!" Ivy joked in a manner not entirely funny. "Perhaps we can finally move into a bedroom upstairs."

Imagine our disappointment when, upon arriving, we found the place in exactly the condition we had left it. That evening's paint-watching felt particularly grueling.

It's not that they're lazy. We hear them every day, pounding, sawing, mixing cement and hammering nails. It's just that we don't know what, in heaven's name, they are doing. While one guy paints arches, another digs trenches in the yard. And as someone else spends his day mixing cement, a fourth worker busies himself fiddling with masses of tangled and multicolored electrical wires.

In fairness, the work completed so far is acceptable. And occasionally, we even see a breakthrough; all the windows are now paned with glass, and they finally installed the long-awaited generator. But the progress still seems agonizingly slow as we watch each chip of paint crystalize into its ultimate and final form.

A Filipino friend with experience in such matters suggests we lock all the workers in a single room and lose the key until it's done. "That way," he says, "you force them to focus."

We are, in fact, considering it.

As we enter the third year of construction and third month of occupancy, however, we are trying to get some focus ourselves; especially on ways of living with this achingly slow pace of progress. Perhaps we need to think of it as a kind of Zen. Instead of watching the paint dry, we need to embrace its wetness. Instead of banging our heads against an imaginary wall we wish was there but isn't, we need to stop envisioning the wall altogether and accept the concept of emptiness. Learn to flow with the state of limbo our lives have become; a seemingly endless lethargy with down as up and up as down, and all other directions going nowhere.

Or... we could schedule another evangelical revival meeting with our esteemed engineer to set some deadlines. First one: getting out of this damn stuffy basement full of ants and into a proper bed.

25
A DEATH IN THE FAMILY

Nov. 1, 2018

I didn't remember him until I saw him dead. His name was Junelito S. Villondo, but friends called him Juni for short. Nearly every day for a year, Juni had come to our house in Punta Bilar as one of dozens of workers charged with making it home. His specialty: stainless welding and metalwork. Last week, our engineer mentioned in passing that Juni had called in sick. Yesterday we went to his funeral.

What happened in the interval, unfortunately, is an all-too-common story in the Philippines. What could happen next, tragically, is even less uncommon.

According to his wife, Juni came home one night complaining of back pains and fever. The next day he was having trouble breathing, so they rushed him to the hospital where doctors made a grim discovery: seething with pneumonia, Juni's lungs had almost entirely filled with water. His life might have been saved by emergency surgery, but his family lacked the funds. So, in a desperate last-ditch effort to keep him breathing, doctors performed a tracheostomy, inserting a tube deep into his windpipe. Writhing in agony, Juni ripped it out and, a few hours later, was dead. Besides his wife, he leaves a 12-year-old daughter, 8-year-old son, and another baby girl on the way. He was 36, and their only means of support.

Sitting at the funeral parlor next to his open casket, Juni's family described his early life. It had been difficult, they said, involving lots of drugs and gang violence. His formal education had stopped after third grade. And yet, somehow, he beat the odds by learning a trade, perfecting his craft, and finding work that paid enough to support a family.

My only clear memory of Juni is watching him install the metal bars encircling a balcony in our upstairs master bedroom. I remember being impressed by his diligence; the slow, methodical way in which he performed the task one step at a time, never hurrying, never doubting his own judgment as his dark penetrating eyes focused entirely on the object of his labor. Wow, I remember thinking, with workers like this, we're in skilled hands.

Now he's gone and someone else will have to finish the job.

The funeral was typically Filipino; in one room sat the widow and children, along with assorted relatives holding a vigil next to Juni's remains. Like widows everywhere, she occasionally smiled fondly at a visitor's recollection of her late husband. Then she'd crumple in tears over his corpse as the reality of what had happened hit home. In an adjacent room, spilling into the yard outside, a crowd of friends and co-workers sat chatting over beer. And I couldn't help feeling that we were a family.

So what will happen to Juni's wife and children without his support? In this culture of poverty, sadly, that remains to be seen. One likely outcome; a younger brother will step in from Cebu to take Juni's place. We would certainly favor that. In the meantime, the rest of us will help as we can. And when I sit on that balcony, I'll think of the man.

26
THE BATTLE OF SURIGAO STRAIT

Nov. 8, 2018

I haven't always been a sucker for national anthems. There was a time, in fact, when I considered strong feelings surrounding nations and their flags to be overly sentimental, even childish, and naïve. Boy, have those times changed. Yesterday, emotion overcame me at the renditions of not one, but *four* national anthems all in a row: Philippines, United States, Australia, and Japan.

The occasion was the 74th annual commemoration of the Battle of Surigao Strait at the Lipata ferry terminal just down the road. They filled the grandstand of honor with important dignitaries, including the city's mayor, several council members, a spokesperson for the provincial governor, various esteemed veterans and representatives of the US and Australian embassies, as well as the nation of Japan. And seated right there among them was none other than yours truly, this obscure immigrant writer.

How on earth, you might wonder, did that happen? It's an excellent question, and exactly what I'd be wondering myself if I were you. In fact, it happened for one reason and one reason only; my house overlooks the waters in which the historic battle took place.

That was in 1944, when the battleships of America and Japan played an elaborate game of tag using live ammunition. In the end, Japan limped away gravely injured, turning the tide of the war in the Pacific, and setting the stage for the liberation of the Philippines the following year. Thousands lost their lives, including Americans, Japanese, Australians, and Filipinos. It was the last great naval battle, not only of World War II but of history itself.

We knew none of this when we purchased our lot back in 2013. All we knew then was that the place had the most incredible view we'd ever seen. And that a voice inside us kept whispering "build it here."

It wasn't long, of course, before we began hearing stories about the spot's historic significance. The following year, the Philippine government purchased the lot next to ours to construct a Naval coastal watch station, now manned 24/7 by four Philippine naval officers. It's also guarded by several Army guys charged with providing security for what's considered the gateway to Mindanao. In fact, our house sits on the northernmost point of Mindanao, from which southern Leyte is clearly visible on the distant horizon. And now, directly below and across the road from us, the city is in the initial stages of constructing the future Battle of Surigao Strait Memorial, a magnificent structure overlooking the water that will eventually include a museum, memorial wall, and flag poles displaying the colors of all four nations involved. It was the solemn raising of those colors that most stirred me during yesterday's ceremony at the terminal.

It wasn't patriotism that moved me, but a new appreciation for the sacrifices of the past; a mournful recognition regarding the significance of those long-ago events and of the place I now live. The keynote speaker was a man named David Mattiske, a 93-year-old Australian World War II veteran and one of the last surviving participants in the Battle of Surigao Strait. "Let us pray," he said, "that we never have another world war."

Next year's commemoration, I'm told, will be at the shrine itself. But tonight, as I peer through my window into the dark waters beyond, I can't help but feel a kinship with the men who fought and died here. They, truly, are the ghostly guardians of the gates that hug my house.

27
A CARIDAD HALLOWEEN

Nov. 15, 2018

I have always had mixed feelings regarding Halloween. While it's certainly fun watching pint-sized witches and goblins beg for treats, the holiday has become increasingly commercialized, especially in the West. In the United States, in fact, it has developed into a thinly veiled excuse for adults to dress up in skimpy costumes and consume large amounts of alcohol.

In the Philippines, the story is different; while most have heard of Halloween, its customs have not yet taken root. This year my sweet wife did her best to change that.

First, some background. When Ivy initially arrived in the US as my fiancé in 2008, she knew precious little about Halloween. Wanting to be a good wife and loyal American, however, she embraced it entirely. We quickly formed the habit of observing the holiday by attending costume parties put on by our friends. Later, after most of those friends—including us–had become parents, the parties grew into elaborate affairs involving door-to-door trick-or-treating with the kids. In fact, Ivy enjoyed it so much that she kept all her costumes.

Ok, fast forward to the present; now we're in the Philippines about to experience our first Halloween abroad. There aren't too many parties in Surigao. So Ivy comes up with an idea; why not bring Halloween to the province? Specifically, to Caridad, the tiny thatched-roof village on Siargao Island where she was born and much of her family still lives.

The two-hour boat ride over is uneventful, except for the novelty of dragging along a large bag of slightly used Halloween costumes. Fortunately,

Ivy's relatives love the idea and so, in no time flat, have decked themselves out as various entities including a bumblebee, cowgirl, Spiderman and witch. I am invited along as the expedition's official photographer. Oh, and there's one other small twist: instead of knocking on doors asking for candy, this troupe of oddly dressed vagabonds will distribute it by the plateful to children in the streets.

And their numbers don't disappoint. At first, of course, one can see a certain puzzlement on their childish faces; what, they are clearly wondering, are these weird, strangely dressed adults doing in our village? Ah, but then they realize that there's sugar involved. And as word quickly spreads, so does the excitement.

"*Ate* Ivy, *Ate* Ivy!" some yell, holding out their hands as the candy flies. And within minutes, I swear, a crowd of at least fifty young ones is following us through the streets as we make our tour of the barangay. The candy supply doesn't last long, but inspires lots of smiles.

Which were the last things I expected at the local cemetery during All Souls Day observances the next day. There were certainly somber moments. As when the priest performed mass, sprinkling holy water on the graves. And the family performed its own prayer at the tomb of Ivy's grandfather. There was also evidence of care, as children lit candles to honor the dead and a young man painstakingly repainted the inscription on a departed loved-one's grave.

But—and this is what surprised me—the overall mood was not one of sadness, but of celebration. It was like a family reunion, filled with laughs and stories about beloved relations dearly departed. Various family groups sat together under makeshift shelters, sharing jokes and the latest gossip. And at least one celebrant appeared to be heavily under the influence of—wait—alcohol?

Hmm, not that different, I guess, from a typical Halloween in California. Minus the skimpy costumes.

28
THE DISAPPEARANCE

Nov. 22, 2018

We met, I suppose, in the usual way, for the beginnings of such relationships. If there *is* a usual way. And if there have *been* such relationships. He was sitting in front of Gaisano Mall with his hand out. I was walking with my 7-year-old son in tow.

"Daddy," my boy said, "what does that man want?"

It was as if a bag of cement hit me. For my immediate instinct had been to look away and hurry on past. But now my son was watching, and that changed the game.

"He wants money," I explained as carefully as I could. "He needs it because he's poor." I reached into my pocket and withdrew all the loose change I could find, perhaps twenty pesos' worth. "Here, Isaac," I said, handing him the money. "Why don't you give him this?"

And that's how it started; a seemingly innocuous relationship that didn't appear to be deep. I never expected to feel so distraught when it suddenly ended a few months later. Sometimes, I guess, the things you take for granted are the ones that hit the hardest.

I should probably add here that Surigao City's main mall—specifically its internet café—is where I spend a part of almost every day. So as the days passed, and I continued seeing the man I thought of as the Gaisano Beggar, well, we gradually developed a routine. At first, it was as innocuous as I considered our relationship. He would simply hold out his hand at my approach and I would fill it with whatever spare change I could muster.

Then things changed. He would see me approaching from a distance and smile. Eventually, if I'd given him something on the way in, he'd refrain from asking later as I passed him going the other way. The message was simple; *You've already done your part today*, he seemed to be saying, *so I won't bother you for any more. Have a good day...*

Sometimes I'd even gesture that I didn't have any change at the moment, and he'd nod in apparent understanding.

Then came the ultimate exchange, a moment that turned out to be the apex of our relationship; he uttered "thank you" in English. It was the first time the Gaisano Beggar had ever spoken to me. And the last: The next day the eagerly outstretched hand was nowhere to be seen.

At first, I thought it a fluke. Perhaps the rain had dissuaded him, or he was feeling ill. I tried to imagine where my friend-of-the-many-fingers lived. Did he have a wife and family waiting for him at home, eager for the day's meager earnings? Did they all sleep together under a bridge downtown?

As the days passed, curiosity turned to alarm. Perhaps the mall's management had banned him from the site. Maybe they'd even had him arrested. Or, worse, was he lying dead somewhere in the middle of a road?

It was then I reflected on what had transpired. For somehow this poor man had gotten under my skin, become part of my life, grown into a fixture and an object of anticipation. He had become an anchor where anchors were achingly few. And I realized how ironic it is that so many of our anchors are invisible until they disappear.

I still look for him. Perhaps one day, I shall experience the exquisite relief of seeing my friend again. I hope that day comes soon.

29
MOVING UP

Nov. 29, 2018

You can't ask a visitor to sleep on the floor. So I recently had a heart-to-heart talk with the engineer overseeing the construction of our house. "You can't ask a visitor to sleep on the floor," I said. "We need to finish the three guest rooms and dirty kitchen by Tuesday."

A dirty kitchen, for those unfamiliar with rural life in the provincial Philippines, is an outdoor facility constructed in most homes specifically for preparing such delicacies as what foreigners refer to as "stinky fish."

As always, our engineer seemed very accommodating. "Of course," he said, "your wish is my command." Or, at least, that's what it sounded like to my eager foreign ears.

So you can imagine my surprise and dismay upon discovering, after returning home late Monday, that the bathroom had no hot water or mirror over the sink and its shower merely dribbled rather than poured. And all this after spending a frantic afternoon moving beds, buying mattresses, and getting the air conditioning units to work, all of which we'd expected to have done weeks before.

I should probably pause here to remind you of some pertinent background. For the past four months, Ivy, Isaac and I have been living in a tiny dusty room in the cockroach-infested basement of our soon-to-be-beautiful mansion-by-the-sea while workers complete the upper floors. The plan has always been to move up into a guest room one level higher the minute our crew gives the word. Then, when they complete the third level, we will elevate ourselves grandly to the master bedroom upstairs.

The problem is that all of it is taking way too long. And now there's a complication: the imminent arrival of our very first guest from abroad, whose plane will touch down on Tuesday. A friend from California named Kathy, she will require, at the very least, a warm bed and shower that will do more than spit at her.

So late Monday night, I frantically sent the engineer a text message expressing my grave concerns. "I am gravely concerned," the text message said. His response was immediate, though not entirely reassuring. "Not to worry," he replied, or words to that effect, "I'll swing by in the morning and take care of everything."

There followed what, for me, was a long dark night of the soul. What it came down to is this; at this late stage in life, why am I living in chaos? And more to the point, when, if ever, will the chaos end? These are questions that never bothered me in my twenties. But now I am a man nearing 70 who's spent half his retirement savings, and for what? To awaken in a cramped room with his clothes stored in boxes? To helplessly stand by as vast multitudes of seemingly immortal ants make off with anything left on the folding platform we call a dining table?

And now the thin veneer of triumph we so carefully constructed for those we love back home who bid us adieu with sighs of envy would soon melt to liquid, destroyed by the relentless wide-eyed gaze of a visitor who would see our lives as they really are.

I slept extraordinarily little.

Then everything changed. Our army of workers arrived at 8 a.m. sharp and, within an hour, fixed all the flaws. And, almost simultaneously, Kathy texted us that the airline had canceled her flight because of a looming typhoon that would leave her stranded in Cebu for at least a few days.

The feared catastrophe had miraculously evaporated. Which just goes to prove the truth of the ancient Filipino maxim that, no matter what happens and despite overwhelming evidence to the contrary, everything will turn out fine.

Ah, but the best news is that we have finally escaped from the dark confines of that infernal ant-cursed basement.

God is good!

30
THE LOST GRAVE

Dec. 6, 2018

It was as if somebody dropped a burning matchstick onto my lap. First there was surprise, then the almost instant and irresistible urge to stand up. Without further ado, I jumped to my feet. "Wow," I said, "let's get to that graveyard right now!"

The cemetery in question is the sole receptacle for corpses in the town of General Luna. For the uninitiated, that charming little hamlet–commonly called GL for short–is a well-known icon of Siargao Island, a teardrop-shaped gem-of-a-landmass off Mindanao's northeastern coast about which I have written before. The most famous site in GL is Cloud Nine, named after an American candy bar; a surf break that *Surfer Magazine*, in the early 1990s, dubbed one of the "ten best surf trips of all time." So, ever since then, surfers from around the world–and, more recently, non-surfing tourists as well–have been flocking to Siargao in droves.

Recently, Ivy and I joined the flock to celebrate GL's fiesta. As is true for most such events, this one featured lots of *lechon*, alcohol, good company, and various other treats. There was also a friend there who blurted out that she knew the location of Mike Boyum's grave.

Let me explain. As is befitting of anyplace with a colorful history, Siargao is rife with legends, and one of the more intriguing ones has to do with an early American surfing entrepreneur named Mike Boyum who helped put the place on the map. According to Wikipedia, he was also a convicted drug smuggler who spent his last years hiding out in GL where, in

1989, he died after a self-imposed 44-day "spiritual cleansing fast." Other accounts claim someone murdered him for the ill-gotten cash he reportedly kept stashed in his mattress.

To be strictly accurate, our friend–who was born and raised in GL–didn't know Boyum's name. She had, however, heard of an eccentric American surfer who died under mysterious circumstances and now lay buried near the grave of her father. Who, incidentally, had died when an opponent in his race for barangay captain several years earlier had shot him in the head. But, hey, that's a whole other story.

"Can you take us to the American's grave?" I asked.

"Of course," she said, and off we went.

Anyone who's ever explored a cemetery in the provincial Philippines will tell you it's like playing a game of *Where's Waldo*. First a motorcycle ride, followed by a long walk along the shore until Voila!, seemingly out of nowhere, loomed the first of many tombs. The place looked like something out of an extraordinarily dark dream. Green moss covered the ancient-looking stones, and we had to brush away decades of debris to step over the tightly packed graves. As we traipsed among them, squinting our eyes to make out the names engraved on the stones, my excitement grew. Could this really be the ultimate resting place of such an enigmatic character from the past? How many people before us had visited his grave, and from where had they come?

Suddenly, we arrived at a large, *especially* moldy stone that stopped our friend short. "This is my father's," she announced, "and right behind him lies the surfer."

Eagerly, I moved forward, stepping over the unfortunate would-be barangay captain's grave to kneel before the second stone. The letters were so moldy I could barely make them out. 1-9----91.

Hmm, I thought, not the right year, but close. Perhaps they'd made a mistake. Maybe they hadn't buried him immediately and recorded the wrong date of death. Carefully, I brushed the dust and mold away from the rest of the inscription to make out the words. They were almost indecipherable, but gradually the letters came into view; R... u... d... *Rudi J. Bischof*! My heart sank; it wasn't him.

But then whose grave was I looking at? Was it possible, I wondered, that more than one wayward surfer on Siargao had come to an untimely end? Did Bischof know Boyum; had they spent time together braving the waves and snorting the snuff? Was this another early adventurer that legend forgot?

And then it struck me as right, at least for today, to leave those questions unanswered. For legend needs mystery, and islands need legend. Better not to uncover too quickly what time had obscured. Better to let mystery spread like the shadow of the moon before disintegrating in the morning light.

As we walked back towards our waiting motorbikes, I felt a sense of disappointment tinged with excitement. Perhaps we would find the lost grave another time. Of one thing I was certain; we would never stop trying.

31
TREES

Dec. 13, 2018

For me, it's all about the trees. Six of them. For many years, certainly as long as I can remember, they've been standing in the large coconut grove owned by my wife at Magpupungko Beach on Siargao Island. They have provided shade, beauty and, yes, the occasional refreshing taste of coco juice sipped right from the shell. Today they are being cut down and my heart is breaking.

Of course, I understand why. For several years now, Siargao has been experiencing a boom in tourism. And Magpupungko, long a haven for locals wishing to bathe in its fabulous saltwater pools, has become a major attraction.

The first time I stood on this beach in 2006, it was the most pristine thing I'd ever seen; nothing but white sand, clear water, gorgeous curling waves and coconut trees as far as the eye could see. The next year we erected what was literally the first structure on the beach; a small cottage near the water's edge for family picnics and gatherings with friends. Between its rafters, cut indelibly into the ceiling, a large heart bore witness to our burgeoning new love. Today, the cottage languishes in disrepair, a relic of the past forgotten by everyone but us.

Once we planned to build our house here. Tucked neatly within range of the ocean's salty smell, we imagined idling away the hours gazing out at the gurgling sea for the rest of our lives. Then things changed; as the wave of tourists grew, our desire to live on Siargao shrank. That, combined with the myriad of boundary disputes breaking out like measles all over the island, inspired a change of plans; instead of building a house, we contented ourselves with a cozy little cabin for weekend getaways.

And that's where the doomed trees come in. One of Ivy's dreams since childhood has been to build a modest resort on her 7,200-square-meter lot-by-the-sea, and recent events seem to indicate that now is the time. At first, I opposed cutting down any trees at all. But as our discussions continued, I gradually succumbed to the evidence until the family persuaded both of us that some of our beloved trees would have to go, not only to make space for the new cabins but to provide wood for their construction. The final number, after going through an arduous permitting process, was six.

Neither Ivy nor I, however, realized how hard it would be. We learned that this morning, as the eager crew of tree cutters arrived to do its work. For a while, I watched with a sinking heart as those loyal, long-serving boughs fell. Then retreated to a nearby porch to write this account with the roar of chainsaws still drilling in my head. Just now, Ivy–unable to watch any longer–came and sat down beside me. With tears in our eyes, we hugged each other and promised to cut no more trees.

Had someone called me a tree hugger back in the US, I'd have found it deeply offensive. Here, somehow, the label fits perfectly.

32
A BARANGAY CHRISTMAS

Dec. 20, 2018

The sight that won me over was the man riding the broomstick with a coconut on his head. Or maybe it was the group of women frantically massaging a phallic rod of fast-melting ice. Whatever it was, I came home from my first barangay Christmas party last night with an entirely new take on the day Christ was born.

I've never been a fan of Christmas parties. It's not just that I'm Jewish. My problem with holiday gatherings is that too often they are stilted affairs imposing forced enactments of merriment and joy.

Not in the Philippines. It didn't hurt, of course, that the barangay captain, spotting us hovering timidly at the entrance of the gymnasium in which he emceed the event, immediately came over to introduce himself and usher us directly to the head table. Nor did his gift of a large bottle of spirits go unappreciated.

Ivy thinks he did all that to encourage our financial participation in this and future events. Which is perfectly fine with me because what I saw in that gymnasium struck me as a colorful celebration of life and community brimming with frolicking fun.

First came the games, everything from wild dance fests pitting block against block to the familiar sack races involving the coconut-hobbled warrior and screaming ice-crazed wives. There were several synchronized dance performances by local groups that had obviously practiced. One group that obviously hadn't was the uniformed barangay police squad dangling over each other like yoyos on strings. And, finally, there was the complete abandonment of all dignity in favor of general disco madness led off by none other than yours truly and his lovely wife.

"Pst!" Ivy said, awaking me from an almost hypnotic gaze previously unpenetrated by human words. "They want us to dance. First *us*, then everybody else."

"But..." I objected as she dragged me onto the dance floor. Suddenly we were dancing with everyone looking on. And that's when I realized that, truly, this is our town.

In fact, hometown is what it was all about. It's like this: virtually everyone in the world longs for the intimacy and familiarity that comes with living in a small community. But the trend in most places is exactly the opposite; more and more people inhabiting larger and larger cities growing increasingly impersonal with each passing day. The Philippines has solved that problem ingeniously by assigning every person in every city to what essentially amounts to a small neighborhood community, namely their barangay. Thus, every Filipino has a real hometown.

That's the perspective that awakened me last night as I watched the faces all around, lost in excitement and fun. Like any small town, our barangay has its own cast of characters, including the town drunk, teenage dreamboat, and local parish president, whose participation in the Christmas gala included publicly reminding revelers to attend mass at 4 a.m.

The town also has its own legends and dramas. Such as the foreigner who drunkenly threatened people with guns, and the guy who recently attempted to steal a motorcycle in broad daylight with no way get its engine started. Both ended up in the town pokey as guests of those bad-dancing cops.

Bottom line: I think I'm going to like it here.

33
A TOOTH IN MY POPSICLE

Dec. 27, 2018

We had just started eating dessert at our favorite restaurant when I bit into something hard. "Wow," I exclaimed incredulously after examining the discarded contents on my plate. "Someone's tooth is in my popsicle!"

What I didn't yet realize was that the delinquent tooth was mine.

That was the beginning of a misadventure resulting in my first encounter with Philippine dentistry. Before telling you about that strange experience, however, let me just, uh, "fill" you in.

We had stopped for lunch in the barangay next to ours en route to downtown Surigao City. Upon finishing, it being an exceptionally hot day, we both decided we were in the mood for something cold. Frozen popsicles were the only dessert they had, not necessarily my favorite. But, what the heck, it was certainly cold and, as we soon discovered, hard as rock.

"Oh goodness," my dear wife said, "don't bite down on this, just take a lick."

"Nah," I said, quickly dismissing her suggestion, "I like the taste of the mush sliding down my throat."

Then I bit in. It felt like any other bite; my teeth penetrated the frozen material with what seemed like the normal amount of pressure. It was, however, the next bite–which, regrettably, turned out to be my last on this dessert–that ended in the aforementioned jaw-jamming halt.

Staring at the cold popsicle mush I had regurgitated all over my plate, I felt suddenly stunned. For there, oddly suspended in its middle, lay a lonely, orphaned tooth. Geese, I thought, is this place careless enough to leave a random tooth stuck in its food? Only in the Philippines. Then my wife suggested I check my mouth.

OK, I understand that I'm getting older. And as one ages, of course, strange things happen to one's body. But I had felt no pain, nor even heard a crack. The bite had seemed successful in every respect. And yet I couldn't ignore the rock-solid evidence now staring me in the face; that there was a tooth on my plate and, yes, in the upper left quadrant of my mouth, a gaping hole.

Moving slowly, I picked up the dead-looking thing and stuck it into the hole. It fit perfectly. Apparently, the darn bit of organic enamel had snapped cleanly off just above the root. My first inclination was to cry. Ivy's, fortunately, was exactly the opposite. And so my dear wife and I concluded our lunch date in uncontrollable peals of laughter.

Ok, pan forward several weeks. I'm sitting in the dentist's chair of someone whose name I've never heard. We'd found him simply by walking into the lobby of the Surigao Medical Center and asking the security guard if there was a dentist on board. Now I'm sitting in his chair while he's thoughtfully stroking his chin.

His first reaction had been to chuckle and remark that "well, the root's still intact so you're in no immediate danger. But eventually you should probably do something about it."

Now he appears to be having second thoughts. "Tell you what," he says, "let me extract that root and put in a denture."

"You mean, like, something I'll have to take out and keep in a glass of water at night?"

"Only when you brush your teeth," he confidently assures me.

But I'm having visions of my fake yellow tooth sitting in that glass on the sink as my beautiful young wife steps up to brush her own lovely white teeth. Oh my God, I'm thinking, now she'll really know I'm old.

The dentist senses my discomfort and quickly offers an alternate plan. "Ok," he says, reaching for his pliers, "we'll make it a bridge; only 16,000 pesos (around $300) and I'll pull that root out now..."

But I am put off by his eagerness. Apparently, so is Ivy, whose searing glances from across the room are about to set the place on fire. Without discussing it, we mumble our excuses and make for the door, though not before succumbing to his insistence on a 2,800-peso deposit for the bridge that we both already know we will never cross.

You've probably guessed by now that we eventually made other plans that involved gingerly stepping–though definitely not *jumping*–off that proposed dental bridge. I'll spare you the details; let's just say that my wounded mouth again feels whole.

But here's the moral of the story, and I know you know it's right; always listen to your wife when she tells you not to bite.

34
OUR HOUSE IS A VERY, VERY, VERY FINE HOUSE

Jan. 3, 2019

The thing about our house is that it has an echo. More of a rumble, really. If you're on the second floor and need someone whose whereabouts is unknown, you simply stand in the middle of the room and yell their name out as loud as you can. Your voice will reverberate through the building, literally bouncing off the walls and ceilings until, eventually, you'll hear a distant response such as "I'm upstairs," "I'm downstairs" or, "I'm in the bathroom, leave me alone."

For a long time I didn't notice it, at least not enough to comment. Then yesterday, a visiting friend got a call from her son. "Are you in the big house?" he asked, "because I can hear the echo."

That our friends and relatives insist on calling it a mansion should have given us a clue. For a long time we objected, insisting that a mansion was decidedly not the thing in which we lived. But they persisted until finally we stopped arguing and hit on an acceptable compromise; what we live in, we now all agree, is a nice little *mansionette*.

For the record, we never intended to build a mansionette. Our plans called for a simple house, but then we found Punta Bilar and our modest intentions inflated like a runaway balloon. The thing is, you can't build a shack at an iconic location like this; no, next to the Punta Bilar Lighthouse you've got to build something worthy of the spot.

And so our plans expanded. Not all at once, mind you. We hired an architect and gave him a basic outline that we'd found online. Obviously influenced by the same factors that had already twisted *our* view, he added a few flares of his own, including a driver's room, maid's quarters, and the so-called "music" room. Whatever the heck that is. And, of course, our engineer tweaked the plan even further by adding a spiral staircase leading to an observation tower as high as the lighthouse; several more windows; three balconies and a large walk-in closet with comfort room inside. The result: about 500 square meters of living space—roughly 5,000 square feet— on four levels, including six bedrooms, three bathrooms, an office, music room, balconies, indoor and outdoor kitchens, and a large wrap-around veranda.

The price tag, of course, expanded accordingly; to the equivalent, we expect, of around 15 million pesos, not including the 1.5 million we already paid for the lot on which the house stands. Estimated total: around $344,000 US. That sounds like a lot until you put it in perspective. In Southern California the land alone, assuming one could find it, would cost millions, considerably more than we–or anyone we know–could afford. And after spending that kind of money, who would have enough left over for a bag of cement?

Despite what our new neighbors may think, we have never considered ourselves rich. But here's a secret few appreciate until they get old; in America, if you work steadily for thirty-plus years depositing 5-6% of your salary into a retirement account, well, you can end up with a fair amount of money at the end of the road. Hopefully, even a little before that final dead-end when you turn 59 ½ and can withdraw it without penalty. Add to that the proceeds from selling a California condo that literally doubled in value in a few years, move to the Philippines and, well, you have your dream mansionette by the sea.

Despite outward appearances, however, the thing is still far from finished. Currently, we remain in one of the guest rooms on the second floor while the construction crew works on the level above. Oh, and finishes the indoor kitchen while we rely on the "dirty" one outside.

One day, they will finish, of course, and the sounds of hammers and saws will be a distant memory. For now, though, I content myself with sitting on the veranda overlooking the glistening sea with my arm around my sweetheart's shoulder as we listen to the soothing strains of an old song recorded by Crosby, Stills and Nash:

I'll light the fire while you place the flowers
In the vase that you bought today
Come to me now and rest your head for just five minutes
Such a cozy room, the windows are illuminated
By the evening sunshine
Fiery gems for you, only for you...

It is those fiery gems, these days, that light my soul.

35
YELLOW DOG

Feb. 3, 2019

Her name was Sandy. For the past five months, ever since we moved here, she'd been yelping in happiness when she saw us come home, protecting us from other stray dogs in the neighborhood and easing my eight-year-old son's transition by cozying up to him each day after school.

Like almost every other dog I've seen in Mindanao, Sandy's color was a bright shade of yellow. Unlike some, she also had a bright disposition; sweet, friendly, protective, and emotional. Today, a speeding car killed her in front of our house and the construction crew across the street ate Sandy for dinner.

In fact, it's not the first time I've heard of such a thing. Years ago, as a reporter for the *Los Angeles Times,* I wrote a series of articles about a Cambodian refugee family in Long Beach, California, whose neighbor had gifted them with a young German Shepherd. Instead of treating it as a pet, however, they'd quickly slaughtered the poor animal and put it on the stove. That's when the police arrived to arrest them for animal cruelty.

The resulting trial was fascinating. The unfortunate Cambodians, completely bewildered by the public reaction to their deed, hired an attorney who presented a cultural defense. In rural Cambodia, he suggested, eating dogs was quite the custom; how were his clients to know that Americans held the animals in such high esteem?

In the end, the judge dismissed the case because he could find no broken laws. But the public uproar was deafening; the defending attorney received death threats and bumper stickers began cropping up around town reading

"Save a Dog, Eat a Cambodian." Finally, a group of dog-lovers, spurred to action by all the publicity, successfully sponsored legislation legally preventing California dog owners from eating their pets.

In the course of my reporting, naturally, one question that arose was precisely which nationalities harbored such unthinkable culinary habits. A leader in the Cambodian community assured me that, in his country, the only citizens with a taste for canines were uneducated peasants. A Vietnamese representative was quite insistent that none of his countrymen would *ever* do such a thing. But the subject of Filipino eating habits never arose.

Now my *Pinay* wife tells me that, though she has never tasted it herself, the consumption of dog meat here is not uncommon. A 19-year-old niece admits to having eaten a mutt that her parents once bought for that purpose. And today the foreman of our work crew met us at the gate with a look of concern on his face.

"There's good news and bad news," he announced immediately. "Which would you like to hear first?"

The bad news, of course, turned out to be that Sandy was dead. The good news: that a group of hardworking fellows was feeling well fed.

Sandy wasn't actually ours; technically she belonged to the crew of Navy guys stationed next door. But from the day we arrived, she seemed as comfortable with us as with them. At night, she would curl up like a lion on her favorite mound guarding the road from our yard. Recently, Sandy's official owners promised my young son one of her puppies. And whenever a stray dog wandered too close to the house, Sandy would take off in pursuit with an angry flurry of barks.

She did that one too many times this morning, chasing a strange interloper into the street directly in front of passing traffic. Unfortunately, while the unknown intruder escaped unharmed, his noble pursuer got flattened by a car. Which has left us pondering what the world will be like without our dear Sandy.

One thing it will be for sure is a lot quieter. But it will also, we are just now realizing, be a lot emptier. I don't begrudge the men who ate our favorite dog; they didn't kill her and at least her death served a purpose. All sentimentality aside, hardworking construction crews need to eat too.

But there's a question that keeps nagging at me and won't go away. I hope you won't think less of me for spitting it out here: just how did Sandy taste? Was she sweet and succulent as when she snuggled up to my child, or hard and nasty as when she chased away her rivals? In the end, I suppose, that will just have to remain one of life's great mysteries lurking here among the howling dogs.

Like why, oh why, are all of them yellow?

36
SEVENTY

Feb. 12, 2019

My seventieth birthday came like a thief in the night. Instead of robbing me, though, it filled me with riches. And now I am a man left counting his blessings.

The day began in the pre-dawn darkness with a choir of young Filipinos serenading outside my bedroom window before handing me a dozen roses. It ended over twenty hours later in an energetic living room dance reminiscent of the days when disco was king. Set between those two bookends was a love fest the likes of which I seldom have seen.

Where I come from, 70 is old. So old that, as a young man, I could hardly imagine ever reaching that age or, if I did, that life would still be worth living. So old that when my father died at 72, I honestly felt he had lived long enough. So old, that I sometimes scoffed at men that age walking hobbled with canes.

Here in the Philippines, it's a whole different story. The native language contains titles of respect automatically bestowed on someone whose age exceeds yours, ranging from older siblings to aunts, uncles, parents, and grandparents. When a Filipino child approaches an adult, he customarily touches the older person's hand to his own forehead in blessing. And though official *legal* senior status is available only to Philippine citizens, no one has yet asked me for an ID when standing in the elder lines at the local Jollibee.

What it comes down to is respect; natives of my newly adopted country simply *respect* age rather than scorn it. I had, of course, long been told of the general Asian deference toward age. But hearing of it and experiencing it are quite different things, especially when the elderly person they're respecting is *you*.

So how did all this translate at my recent birthday bash? The setting, of course, was our new home overlooking the ocean, where the party had begun the night before with twenty relatives from Siargao Island. As usual, they all slept on the floor in a writhing mass of heads, arms, torsos, and legs. The next morning, while some set about decorating the place with balloons and fancy tablecloths, others mounted an enormous poster bearing several likenesses of yours truly over the caption "Happy 70th Birthday, David Haldane."

"You look so handsome!" one 19-year-old niece sighed.

By the time the guests began arriving later that evening, the drinking had long since begun.

So how to describe the next several hours? There was, of course, the usual orgy of imbibing, dancing, and carousing. There were also several toasts to my longevity and health, and a series of well-staged photo ops with me, my wife, and our eight-year-old son. And there was a table strewn with Filipino delights such as *ube, pancit,* an array of colorful seafoods and a stout pig who'd arrived squealing in a sack ready for gutting and roasting. The caterers later said they ran out of food after loading 150 plates. And lest there be any lingering doubt, let me just say that not once–even for a *split second*– did I ever feel old.

In a conversation about aging earlier that day, my 36-year-old wife said, "I look forward to it. I can hardly wait for the time when I have all that knowledge and experience."

And there, my friends, lies the essential Filipino attitude toward aging; rather than dread, they embrace it with anticipation. Pretty wise for such a young country. And not too terrible a place for an old guy like me.

37
ANTS, RATS, LIZARDS, AND SPIDERS

Feb. 18, 2019

For the longest time, I thought it was me. I'd be lying in bed, just dropping off the sleep, when suddenly a tiny yellow lizard would scamper across the ceiling above my head. Or I'd walk into the kitchen just in time to see a huge brown spider slithering up its wall.

"Geez," I'd say to Ivy, "we've got to do something about these critters!" What I neglected to tell her, of course, was that I'd *already* done something about that darn spider with a little help from my shoe.

"Sure, honey," she'd respond sweetly, "no worries, we will." But I could never escape the feeling that I was being placated. And, of course, nothing ever eliminated the varmints inhabiting our house and eating our food.

One night, she calmly informed me that a rat was living in our bedroom. She knew that, she explained, because she'd just seen the thing scurrying across the floor. What surprised me, though, was the tone in which she spoke; the same she would use in offering a morning cup of coffee. That's when I realized the problem wasn't *how* we lived, but *where*.

See, the Philippines is what Westerners politely refer to as a developing nation. That label, of course, has lots of connotations, including poor roads, crowded conditions, and a general lack of infrastructure. Oh yes, and toilets that don't flush with showers that won't heat. Now I was experiencing firsthand yet another drawback that hadn't previously occurred to me; tiny creatures running amok.

"I guess this is just something we'll have to make peace with," I told Ivy, stroking my chin thoughtfully. "I mean, there's a definite *price* you pay for living in a country like this, certain things you have to give up. But, gosh, there must be *something* we can do about these bugs."

A few weeks later, I experienced an event that completely changed my perspective. Ivy and I attended a fancy wedding reception downtown. Perhaps you're wondering how something as mundane as that could have a life-changing impact, so let me be specific; what did it was the *table* at which we sat. It was nice-looking, lovingly strewn with an array of Filipino delicacies, including roasted bananas, crispy pork, barbecued chicken, and fried fish, to name just a few. The table was also crawling with ants.

It's not as if they were eating our meal; a protective plastic wrap made the food exceedingly challenging to reach. Not for lack of trying, though; as I watched incredulously, the tiny army of ants scrambled up over the plastic wrappings and surrounded our plates, spreading like a puddle across the table's surface.

Back home in the US, of course, such a menagerie of insect life–in the unlikely event it survived this long–would, by now, have become a major cause of embarrassment and consternation, resulting in an abject apology by the wedding planner. Not to mention its own immediate annihilation. Much to my astonishment, however, none of my fellow guests seemed to even notice the ants. As if following a secret script, they simply took their respective seats, smiled benignly at each other, and began carefully brushing the insects aside to uncover their food.

That's when it struck me, as suddenly and shockingly as a bolt from the sky: What I had previously taken as a mark of the country's backwardness was, in fact, a sign of its highly evolved culture. To put it simply, Filipinos have made peace with nature. Instead of constantly pitting themselves against it, as we Americans do, they have learned to live in harmony with nature's lowliest creatures, including its ants, rats, lizards, and spiders.

It would be difficult to overstate the effect this revelation had on me. It blew my mind. In short, I began viewing the native inhabitants of my adopted country with newfound respect and a sincere desire to emulate their enlightened behavior. Being American born, of course, it won't be easy, but I have a plan. The next time I see a spider crawling up the wall, instead of grabbing a shoe, I will simply relax and call it my brother.

Hey, it's a start.

38
PINK SKY

Feb. 25, 2019

It was as if the sky had caught fire. The fog rolled in, the sun touched the horizon and, for a few moments–a magical instant in time–the elements intersected to bathe the world in pink. I grabbed my camera and frantically began snapping pictures as the ocean of color surrounded us, oozing in through the windows and doors, forcing its way into our house and our souls.

I had never seen such a thing and wondered what it meant. As the fiery mist settled into the whites of our eyes and the moist, empty spaces of our brains, it felt like a shift. As if there were two realities separated by a thin curtain that nature had suddenly pulled aside, thrusting us into an alternate space where we didn't belong or reside.

I thought of *The Wizard of Oz*, a movie I'd seen repeatedly as a child. There's a scene towards the end where Dorothy, finally facing the much-feared Great and Powerful Wizard, sees him as a huge flaming face barking orders in a thundering voice. But then she pulls aside a curtain, revealing the source of the fiery spectacle as a small meek-looking old man in a control booth pulling strings and speaking into a microphone. "Pay no attention to the man behind the curtain!" the Wizard barks, but it is too late because Dorothy—and the audience—has already glimpsed the reality the curtain hides.

Kind of like a visit we once made to Socorro, a picturesque little town on the coast of a remote and enchanted Philippine island called Bucas Grande. We hadn't planned on stopping there, but halfway to our actual destination–a magical cove where rock formations look like carefully crafted sculptures and the jellyfish have no sting–our small boat sprang a leak and began to sink. We had almost given up hope when a kindly octopus fisherman offered a tow.

Neither of us had ever been to Socorro, nor had we imagined being there now. But the boatman had a cousin in town who offered his floor for the night. And when we asked where to bathe, he pointed up the street as if the answer to our question was obvious. After a long and dusty trudge, we came upon a small fountain carved into a concrete basin at the end of the street. A handful of people sat squatting around it, splashing water onto their faces and arms before erupting in broad smiles induced by the cooling liquid. We quickly joined them, thinking how odd it was to find a public bath in such an out-of-the-way place. It wasn't until years later that we learned the story behind Socorro's renowned bathing basin; that scores of residents had come to violent ends, defending it as a sacred place.

Constructed in the early 1920s by a "holy man" who loved leading followers to mass poolside healing sessions in pre-dawn torchlight processions, the locals soon regarded the fountain as the town's prized possession. So it wasn't surprising that, when colonial authorities ordered it destroyed in 1923, the townsfolk rose in anger, sparking a revolt–widely reported as a "religious war"–resulting in many causalities. So what had appeared to us as a primitive and obscure bathing spot inconvenient and hard to reach, actually glimmered as a living symbol of the town's history, significance, and identity.

We, of course, knew none of this when we first visited the place. Because, for us, all that history was still the reality behind the curtain, the alternate explanation, the unseen story that would have grandly deepened our perspective had someone pulled that curtain aside.

But no one did, just as no one does for most of us most of the time. Only rarely does that magical pink light penetrate our earthly curtain. Living in Mindanao is kind of like that; you recognize the familiar while the strange and unknown remains invisible. Until one day the curtain gives way to the hidden reality it hides.

But here's the thing; you never know when that will happen. And it is the anticipation that keeps you alive.

39
BROKEN

March 5, 2019

Somehow, I knew from the beginning it was too good to be true. A 2015 Yamaha Mio scooter, not a great looker but still in good working order. We'd been talking about getting one for months. The owner wanted 30,000 pesos; we offered him 20,000 and, *bam,* the scooter was ours!

It's hard to overstate the importance of motorcycles in the Philippines, they are truly ubiquitous. By far the preferred mode of transportation, virtually everyone grows up on or near one. Most start riding as passengers in infancy and, by their early teens, are pumping the throttle solo, licensed or not. So it was no surprise that Paula, my wife's 19-year-old niece, was hot to take a spin.

She was living with us in the capacity of what Filipinos call a "working student." In her first year studying electrical engineering at a local college, Paula helped with cooking, cleaning, childcare, and various other chores, in exchange for room and board, tuition, books and daily transportation to school, usually provided in the family van. One thing decidedly not included in the arrangement, however, was the privilege of driving our new scooter. That, I assured her, remained strictly reserved for Ivy and me.

It was on the back of one, in fact, that our romance began. It happened back in 2006 when, after a whirlwind online love affair, I'd made my first tentative sojourn to Surigao City to meet this mysterious dark-eyed woman of my fantasies. Ivy, with a chaperone in tow, met my incoming ferry at the port. Almost immediately, she escorted me to another boat laden with pigs and bananas for the three-hour trip to her birthplace, Siargao Island, for a serious meeting with Mom and Dad. And it was on that island a few days later that the epiphany occurred.

We had borrowed her dad's motorcycle to tour the island, with Ivy driving and me holding on for dear life behind. On one side of the road stood a coconut-tree forest, and on the other a jade-colored sea. As my fingers dug into my future wife's narrow waist with her long black mane streaming luxuriantly back across my face, an overwhelming certainty seized me; that life didn't get any better than this. And, just like that, I embarked on the love that would seal my fate.

So I'm sure you can understand why, thirteen years later, we were more than happy to welcome a motorcycle–even a dim replica of the two-wheeled giant that played such a decisive role in our relationship–back into our lives. And so it was with great joy, and a sort of tingling in my fingers, that I looked forward to taking another ride; this time with Ivy in back and me at the controls.

Then Paula got hold of the thing. We knew immediately that something was amiss when, coming up the driveway happily exhausted after a weekend away, a squad of neighbors met us at the door.

"Uh-oh," I said to Ivy, "this can't be good."

It wasn't. Through an excited jumble of *Bisaya*, hastily translated by my wife, I pieced the story together. Paula, it seemed, had somehow found the key, and taken an unauthorized joy ride on our as-yet untested bike. Now the machine lay crumpled in a heap at the bottom of a nearby hill, and Paula lay in a local hospital bed with a seriously broken arm. Apparently, our informants explained, she'd mistaken the throttle for the brake.

Paula no longer lives with us. Instead, she opted to drop out of school and return home for the duration of her recovery, a solution to which neither Ivy nor I raised a shard of objection.

The future of our beloved bike is still uncertain. Tomorrow we shall take it to the shop to determine whether a mechanic can resurrect the sad machine, or declare it as broken as Paula's arm. In the meantime, our romantic victory lap following more than a decade of marriage is on indefinite hold.

Does the story have a moral? Only this; the brake is on the left and the throttle on the right. That may seem obvious but, in fact, it's profound. For in life, as on motorcycles, one must sometimes slow down.

40
ISAAC'S BOG

March 12, 2019

It happened again the other day. I was at the private school Isaac attends in Surigao City. His second-grade class had just let out and, waiting nearby, I spotted him marching towards me across the grass.

"Hey daddy," he said, "can you carry my bog?

"Excuse me?" I replied, nonplussed. "Your *bog*?"

"My *lunch* bog," he said, without skipping a beat. "I ate nothing, and it's feeling kind of heavy."

I immediately felt my blood rising, as it always does on such occasions. This time, though, I resisted the urge to declare that I didn't know what he was talking about and demand that he pronounce it correctly. Instead, I just grabbed the lunch bag and motioned him toward the car. Perhaps I'm finally making peace with my son becoming Filipino.

Na, just kidding; I hate it now as much as ever.

It's not the heritage to which I object. My Filipino wife and I have always taught Isaac to honor both his Filipino and American sides. No, the part that bothers me—makes me crazy, actually—is my little boy's persistent and annoying insistence on speaking English with a Filipino accent.

It's not as if he doesn't know proper English. Isaac spent the first seven of his eight years in Southern California having long conversations with his American father—namely *me*—and attending an American public school in which English was the only language spoken. He was born in the USA, for heaven's sake, and though his citizenship is dual, his cultural roots are red, white, and blue.

Yet, ever since moving to the Philippines ten months ago, my son has been saying *mom* instead of mam and calling his bag a *bog*. At first, I thought it was just a temporary affectation that would soon disappear. Instead, it seems to get worse with each passing year.

"Daddy," he said the other night from his bed, "my *toblet* is low *bot*; *con* you please close the light?"

Initially, I thought I could just intimidate him into submission. "Sorry," I told him, "but I only respond to requests made in proper English, so please try again."

His mother, who was nearby, however, quickly tucked him in.

To some extent I get it, of course; Isaac is literally the new kid on the block who—not yet fully fluent in *Bisaya*—is trying desperately to fit in. Lately, however, I've noticed that, whenever the subject comes up, he immediately embraces his Filipino side while admitting to the other one only when absolutely pressed. The inescapable conclusion: that my son thinks being Filipino is way cooler than being from the US of A.

All of which, for me, unfortunately, has created a sort of existential crisis. You can believe me when I say I've never been a flag waver. Somehow, though, these recent events—and especially the powerful feelings they have engendered in me—have raised a troubling specter; that, despite my claims of multiculturalism, I am at heart a red-blooded American.

Please don't tell anyone.

41
JEROME

March 18, 2019

His name was Jerome. For about three months, he was our driver. Now he's not, and I am once again reduced to risking my life daily on the streets of Surigao City.

Let me make one thing clear straightaway: I'm not a person accustomed to having his own personal driver. At least not back in the USA, where only the extraordinarily rich can afford such a luxury. But then I moved to the Philippines and the social landscape changed. For a while, I resisted the idea. Until the day our car landed in a roadside ditch from which it escaped only by the good grace of strangers.

Jerome seemed to come out of nowhere; one day he was driving a truck for the construction crew across the street, and the next he was working for us. For 6,000 pesos a month plus room and board, he promised not only to be available for me and my wife, but arise at 6:30 each morning to drive little Isaac to school. Then he sweetened the deal even further; for another 4,000 pesos his wife would cook our meals and clean our house. Oh yes, and wash our clothes too. Bottom line: for a total of roughly $190 US a month, we'd barely have to lift a finger on our own behalf.

Suddenly, life was sweet; no more stumbling groggily out of bed to dodge motorcycles along the city's streets. No more fender benders with errant-yet-fist-shaking tricycle drivers cursing in a foreign tongue. And no more quick trips to the local body shop to cover up mysteriously inflicted scratches and scars.

To fully appreciate the gravity of all this, you need to know something about Surigao streets. They are deadly. Though I am sure there are laws designed to maintain order on them, I have never seen one enforced. What

I *have* seen—usually from way too close—includes motorcycle drivers without helmets or lights transporting seven passengers in the middle of the night, tricycles and pedestrians jumping out at you from unmarked side streets, and children playing in the middle of narrow curvy roads. In a word, it's chaos; a game of chicken that the most daring driver wins. Or loses big time if some other driver has bigger *cajones* that day than his. So you can imagine my relief at finally having someone other than yours truly available to take all that heat.

For a time, all went well; in fact, it went swimmingly. Life, as one famous old nursery rhyme puts it, was a bowl of cherries. And then we started hearing things. Jerome needed an advance to pay his bills. His wife, Justine, was under fire from barangay neighbors for working full time while leaving two young children with Mom and Dad. In the end, that's what did us in. Wilting under the weight of alleged social pressure, Justine quit. And about a week later, Jerome simply stopped coming to work without ever telling us why.

It's not all bad, of course. I no longer suffer the daily awkwardness of being chauffeured by a man who calls me sir. And the basement space once occupied by our resident helpers—dubbed, appropriately enough, the "driver's room" by the apparently prescient architect who drew up our plans—is being refurbished.

But then there are those streets; that infernal network of tangled highways and snarling roads patiently awaiting the chance to snare me in their nightmarish folds. Frankly, I never want to see them again from behind a steering wheel. And, sure enough, just when I thought I might have to, wouldn't you know it, help arrived on a shining white horse in the guise of--my wife?

Yes, it's true, lads, she is now the family chauffeur. But before you make any wisecracks regarding the sorry state of my manhood, listen up; things are different here in the Philippines, including relationships between the genders. Grist, I suspect, for a future column.

42
DOGS, ROOSTERS, AND BAD KARAOKE

April 4, 2019

A howl suddenly awakened me in the night. Somewhere close, a dog was complaining. But it wasn't just an ordinary howl; piercing, mournful and terrifying, the cry in the dark sounded more like a wolf baying at the moon than a hound expressing its discomfort. Soon other dogs—dozens throughout the neighborhood—began answering their unhappy cousin's call with their own discordant symphony of barks, whines, and heartbreaking whimpers. It was only hours later and with much difficulty that I finally got back to sleep. Just in time for a wild cacophony of roosters' crows to awaken me anew.

Anyone who's ever spent time in the provinces of the Philippines knows exactly what I'm talking about; even in Surigao City, the sounds of the night are never too far. I used to think it was mostly animals causing all the ruckus. Then a recent visit with friends in Dalaguete, near Cebu, dramatically pulled aside the curtain of a new quadrant in my understanding. We spent roughly three days with our friends: he, an American like me and she, a Filipina like my wife. And of all those hours, only a few passed unaccompanied by the tone-deaf strains of their most proximate neighbor's wretched attempts to make music. Vastly amplified, of course, by her overly enormous karaoke system.

Please don't misunderstand; I appreciate, and occasionally even indulge in, the universal human impulse to raise one's voice in song. What I've never quite understood, though, is why in the Philippines there seems to be an inverse relationship between the quality of the effort and its volume. The more horrible the voice, the louder the song.

Then I noticed something telling. While our friends were more-than-willing to express their displeasure at the auditory intrusion in the privacy of their own home, the idea of addressing it directly to the offending neighbor—or to *any* neighbor at all—was completely out of the question. All of which started me wondering; in what other national environs can one, without repercussions, keep the neighbors up all night with barking dogs and off-key singing? Certainly not in America, where such behavior would invariably earn you a prompt rap on the door by the local police.

Here's the thing: The Philippines, to be sure, is a developing country, ergo disorganized and often inconvenient. But, ironically, amidst all that chaos—to some extent, in fact, *because* of it—lies something sorely lacking in the more-developed West; *freedom*. And freedom's underlying requirement absorbed into the country's cultural DNA, *tolerance*. While the West—especially the USA—loudly proclaims its devotion to that much-ballyhooed value, it is in increasingly short supply these days in the public lives and private souls of too many befuddled Americans.

And so I find myself in northern Mindanao, where freedom is available for the relatively low price of a few sleepless nights. In fairness, though, the sounds of this land are not always loud and disruptive; sometimes they whisper to you in soothing tones. I first heard that caressing murmur on Siargao Island where, one magical afternoon, I spent a perfect hour in a hammock over the sand, accompanied by a sleeping dog. And the next morning rose early to a child's singing with, yes, a veritable choir of crowing roosters.

That, as I have written before, is when I knew I was home.

43
MY LIFE AS AN ICHTHYOPHOBIC

April 11, 2019

It all started with a fish. I must have been about 7 when my mother laid one on my plate and ordered me to eat it. Instead, I threw up all over the table. And that pretty much sums up my relationship to seafood ever since.

Wait, that's not entirely true. In another life, I was an avid scuba diver who spent weekends and vacations exploring the subterranean worlds of Southern California, Mexico, Honduras, Cayman, Florida Keys, Hawaii, Fiji and, yes, the Philippines. To be sure, there were more than a few sea creatures of various colors and descriptions hanging around those places and, yes, I bid farewell to a fair amount of time, money, and energy trying to get close enough to some of them for personal conversations. Once in Ensenada, Mexico, in fact, I got close enough to shoot one; an act that filled me with such guilt, self-loathing and contrition that I immediately broke the offending speargun over my knee and never used such a weapon again.

I think it was about then I began telling people the reason I didn't eat fish was because they were my friends, but that was a lie. I couldn't eat them because their taste and smell filled me with such overwhelming disgust and loathing that, well, the vomit inevitably followed.

Which, naturally, has not made me an immensely popular dinner guest in Surigao City, where locals take a fair amount of pride in the quality of their ocean cuisine. I realized what I was up against during my first visit to the city's much-touted downtown wet market; a vast expanse of waterlogged wooden tables bearing a greater number and variety of fresh, brightly colored, slimy, squirming, flopping, gyrating, gleaming, odorous seafood than I had ever seen or imagined possible.

"Oh my God," I thought, "what am I doing here?"

The irony of the situation is clear to my Filipino family and friends, whose reactions to my unorthodox culinary habits range from a genuine concern for my health, well-being, and chances of survival to a kind of bemused bewilderment at the amazing wonders which God hath wrought.

Once my wife's parents, upon learning that I might be staying with them briefly while she was away, reacted with genuine panic. "But what will we feed him?" they wanted to know. "What will he eat? We have no food!"

Don't think that I haven't tried changing. A few years ago, keyed up for a complete renewal of life and spirit, I pitched a piece on altering lifelong habits to a popular American magazine. And then, buoyed by a new sense of purpose and professional commitment, forced myself to eat a living—yes, actually *undulating* like a spiny bowl of Jell-O—purple sea urchin at a Japanese seafood restaurant in Huntington Beach, California. Later, my Filipino wife told me she used to do the same with urchins picked off the ocean floor in her hometown of Pilar on Siargao Island. Then she'd crack open their shells and scoop the meat out by hand.

In the end, my magazine article got rejected because, according to the editor, "the average reader won't be able to relate to someone who simply and irrationally hates seafood." And so, I have returned to my previous habit of surviving on chicken, beef, occasionally pork and, yes, a whole lot of salads. Thus, aside from my freakish anti-seafood fetish, life in the Philippines seems almost normal.

Recently, I came across a word for the malaise from which I suffer: *ichthyophobia,* defined by Wikipedia as "fear of fish, including fear of eating fish or fear of dead fish."

Finally, I have a name to blame. Already, I feel much better.

44
THE SACRED POOL

April 25, 2019

At the center of everything lies the pool.

To members of the Atoyay Farmer's Association of Bucas Grande Island, its waters are sacred. It is the holy water they drink and in which they bathe. And it is next to these enchanted godly waters that they make their homes and live their lives.

The placid blue pool forms the shape of a heart fed by a swan-like fountain, but it wasn't always so. Once, in the picturesque town of Socorro on the island's wayward side, a smaller version served as the object of frequent candlelight processions by local townspeople who believed bathing in its blessed waters cured their earthly ills. And it was, as I have previously explained, the arbitrary destruction of that pool by colonial authorities in 1924 that led to the infamous "Colorum Uprising," billed in America as a bloody rebellion by religious fanatics resulting in hundreds of deaths and the torching of the town.

About 3,000 descendants of those so-called fanatics now bathe in a new holy pond at the edge of a 2,300-hectare homestead they call Dizon Village. Recently, I paid them a visit to explore—and, if possible, *experience*—the mysteries of that historic water.

I should probably explain that, perhaps still smarting from the memory of indignities suffered nearly a century ago, these people don't encourage visitors. In fact, the only way I scored an invitation was through my friendship with a noted local historian named Fernando A. Almeda Jr., who wrote about them in his classic, *The History of a Province: Surigao Across the*

Years, and subsequently became a protector. So, it was with some wonderment, that I boarded the boat they provided to take us to their island home.

The first thing you see is the pool. Fed by natural spring waters propelled by gravity through a series of higher ponds built pleasantly into the mountainside, the thing sports an unearthly sparkle that makes you want to blink. They put us up for the night in a building referred to as "the mansion," a majestic hotel-like structure that isn't a hotel at all but a place for their friends. And it was there that Prince Jerrymie Piao—a young man who, like most residents, says he was born here and intends to die here—picked me up for a tour.

Besides the mansion, there's a courthouse, a large room for gatherings and worship, the house of the community's matron who they call *Mommy Lucy* and obey without question, and even a school serving over 300 students ranging from kindergarten through high school with a few university classes thrown in. Its major claim to fame; it's Mindanao's only institute of learning known to teach the indigenous pre-colonial written form of the local language.

The community supports itself primarily through farming, fishing, and carpentry. Though decidedly Christian, its members do not consider themselves Catholic. The major difference, according to my guide, is that no priest-like intermediaries are required to intercede on a worshiper's behalf. And the residents' individual and group prayers were clearly bountiful, wafting in the air both day and night.

But I had come for the water and wouldn't let anything dissuade me. At the town's outer edge, we knelt at a stream and my host bade me drink. The liquid was clear and cool, eagerly flowing down my throat in a soothing waterfall of sensations. But was this truly the water of God, or, like water anywhere, simply rife with the relief of a nagging thirst after an exceedingly long walk?

And then it hit me like a monsoon thunderbolt seen from the comforting wetness of that lovely heart-shaped pool, first distant and then up close; *all* water is the water of God. For without its nourishment we could not survive and without its flow, we surely would languish. My father once told me that if ever I found myself lost in the wilderness, I should follow the water. As it is in the wilderness, so it is in life.

Before returning to the mainland the next day, I spent some time sitting by the sacred pool with my eyes closed, trying to feel its healing powers. I'm not sure I felt them. But the sound of the seawater lapping at the nearby shore was mesmerizing, and the soft ocean breeze cooled my skin like a healing salve.

I don't know whether that pool is holier than any other. What I knew then and know now, though, is that a piece of it stayed with me. And that one day, God willing, I will return it to its source.

45
MANANA

May 9, 2019

The silence was unsettling.

It was 9:30 a.m. on a Monday; not a time usually given, at our house, to the peaceful emptiness of morning reveries. No, at Surigao City's Punta Bilar where we are building our dream home, Monday mornings—in fact, *every* morning save Sunday—usually reverberate with the strangely soothing sounds of hammers crunching nails, saws biting wood and the indecipherable yet jocularly reassuring repartee of construction workers embarking on a day of work.

This day, however, was different; instead of hammers and saws, only the distant braying of dogs disturbed the morning's uncanny calm.

"Is it a holiday?" I asked Ivy.

"Not that I know of," she said.

A few hours and several text messages later, we had unraveled the mystery: our entire construction crew, hung over from a night of drinking at their nearby barangay's fiesta, had taken the day off. "I thought these guys needed the work," I complained to their supervisor who, responding to our urgent request, finally showed up to deliver the bad news in person. "I thought they had families to support."

Taking a deep breath, he explained as best he could. "Well, it's like this," the man began in *Bisaya*. Here is my wife's rough translation of his next several words: in the Philippines, if you have a sack and there's rice in it, even just a little, you stay home. Only when the sack is empty, do you go to work. Which around here is more often the case than not.

OK, before continuing this saga-of-woe, let me make a confession: it had happened before. Once, in fact, after an energetic Christmas party, our entire work crew disappeared, without notice, for more than a week. Which brings us to a sensitive subject, *culture*.

In America, people speak with pride of the "Puritan work ethic," i.e. the pilgrims' sacrifice on which our forefathers built the country. Reduced to its essence, it means you work for as long as you can as often as you can and, if you don't show up one day because you're hung over, well, you get fired. Period, no questions asked.

Contrast that to the Philippines, where so-called "Filipino time"— often a subject of jest—is actually a *real* thing, as anyone who's ever spent any of it here can readily attest. I believe it stems from the country's laid-back Spanish heritage typified by two linguistically related phenomena, both of them frequent and long, *siestas* and *fiestas*. Another country sharing that heritage, of course, is Mexico, which, in the days before America's current orgy of political correctness, often found itself the butt of jokes voiced by unenlightened gringos regarding "manana culture."

Many Americans would argue, perhaps with some justification, that the Puritan work ethic vs. manana culture is one reason the USA has provided perhaps the highest standard of living for the greatest number of people in world history while Mexico and the Philippines are still, well, to put it politely, *developing* nations.

But here's the thing; that's not all bad. While the world considers Filipinos to be among the happiest and friendliest people on the globe, Americans exhibit high levels of stress and depression. They also suffer from disintegrating families, addiction to work, alienation from society and each other, mass violence, annoying outspokenness, and impatient, demanding personalities. Bottom line; like most things in life, it's *complicated*.

Which is why, when Ivy and I noticed our workers putting in full shifts on Labor Day, a public holiday on which, by all rights, they could have called in sick, we wanted to show our appreciation.

"What doesn't cost too much that they would really enjoy?" Ivy wondered.

"I know," I offered, "how about a bottle of Tanduay rum to share after work?"

Our fervent hope: that it won't prevent them from showing up tomorrow.

46
SEALED LIPS

May 16, 2019

The warnings were vociferous.

Strewn among the various online expat forums to which I subscribe, they were stern and concise; avoid potential immigration problems, they declared in unison, by refraining from participation of any kind in the Philippine midterm election. Don't talk about it. Don't acknowledge it. Certainly don't, God forbid, express an opinion. And on election day, one expat warned, make it a point not to venture anywhere near an active polling place lest some otherwise bored government official mistake you for a troublemaker. In fact, he suggested, that might be the perfect day to stay home and read a book.

And so I did.

The warnings, of course, pertained to a government policy well known to expats in the Philippines, specifically that any kind of political involvement by foreigners including taking part in protests, publicly expressing opinions, campaigning on behalf of candidates, or interfering with elections in any way can be grounds for immediate deportation.

All of which amounts to the fact that, with the election over, I feel like I've been holding my breath for a very long time. The funny thing, though, is that I have no desire to exhale. Not that I'd have much to say if I did. My understanding of Philippine politics is far too rudimentary to concoct anything meaningful to add. What I *will* say, however, is that, from the economy seats, this buggy ride has been extremely engaging. Wait, I'll even go a step further. In some ways, it's been inspiring.

That's because I come from America, where democracy has been around long enough to have become an object of almost universal cynicism, derision, and scorn. Accustomed, in the past, to mouthing daily silent mantras designed to summon forth the will and energy to vote, I now live in a country whose citizens routinely and willingly travel hundreds of kilometers to take part in their hometown electoral processes.

Wow. I mean, just *wow*!

It's not perfect, of course, as nothing ever is. One hears stories of electoral corruption on various levels, sometimes even culminating in violence. And there are complaints, as there are everywhere, that some voters do not choose their champions wisely. I am in no position to say whether that is true.

For my money, though, here's the major difference between Filipino-style democracy and the process I've become accustomed to in America, *enthusiasm*. Not, mind you, just the requisite enthusiasm supporters universally show for their chosen candidates. No, what I'm talking about here is a broader kind of enthusiasm, the kind that sustains nations; a deeply rooted, idealistic, excitement-driven, youthful enthusiasm for nothing less than the *process itself*. The sort of enthusiasm that, during the runup to elections, tolerates fleets of slow-moving poster-adorned vehicles blaring eardrum-bursting music between barely audible speeches delivered over barely functional loudspeakers.

What in America—especially in the current political climate—would probably spark riots.

Perhaps that's because democracy in the Philippines is still a shiny new toy, whereas in America it's a torn old book with yellowing pages. Increasingly, it seems, Americans are losing sight of the *process* in favor of the *results*; if your candidate wins, the election was successful and, if not, well, there are always other means.

I don't mind admitting that this scares me, probably because I am old enough to remember the days when elections ended and voters put aside their differences to work for the common good, at least until the next election. That is the cornerstone of democracy and the only way it can work.

So here is my hope for the young democracy I now call home; that it can serve as a gentle reminder to the older one I left behind. That, with this election season over, Filipinos can now unite to move forward in a way that lights up their corner of the globe.

For that is the democratic tradition, one that too many Americans seem to have unfortunately misplaced in the country of both its birth and mine. And that is bad news for us all.

47
BADASS!

May 23, 2019

I think the helmet is what finally did it.

It was a sleek, stylish little model made by Adidas that we'd bought from a street vendor in Vietnam. I slipped it on, grabbed my coolest-looking shades, and threw a leg over the used Yamaha Mios motor scooter we'd recently repaired after the aforementioned mishap involving a niece's broken arm. Then I revved up the engine, gunned it twice, and that was all it took; I was now officially a Filipino badass!

Well, ok, not *entirely* Filipino; my skin was still a little too pasty white for 100% authenticity. But certainly, Filipino *inside* in a way that made me bristle with confidence and newfound pride. For this had been my goal all along, and now I'd finally achieved it!

Perhaps I should explain. My infatuation with everything Pinoy had, in fact, begun on a motorcycle not unlike the one I now rode. That was back in 2006 when, following a whirlwind online romance, I'd made my first trip to Siargao Island to visit the woman of my dreams, who, as I've reported before, took me on an island tour aboard the family bike with her in the driver's seat and me hanging on in back for dear life.

I've spent the last several years, especially since deciding to make the Philippines my home, carefully studying the motorcycle-riding habits of Filipinos. And what I've discovered is that there's one quality all local badasses share: *fearlessness.* The complete confidence that the enormous truck bearing down on you will swerve before you do, and the pedestrian hurrying across the street as you bear down on *him* will get out of the way voluntarily before you put him out of the way for good.

Expressed more crudely, the basic Philippine driving credo is this; he who has the biggest balls, wins. Period. Which, as you might have guessed, presented a major obstacle to yours truly, whose lower anatomy is, well... somewhat less than impressive in that regard.

It didn't help, of course, when Ivy's 19-year-old niece—living with us as a working student—took that unauthorized joy ride on the vehicle in question, resulting in her hospitalization for a broken arm. Nor did my minor excursions on a similar vehicle at about the same age offer much solace or counsel.

And so, I set out to conquer my fears even while wearing out several shoe bottoms in vain efforts to maintain balance when traffic was slow. Sheesh, I honestly thought I'd never make it.

Then, somehow, I did. The unsteadiness lessened and my confidence grew. Until one day I realized I could do the 20-minute drive from our house to the Gaisano Capital mall without even touching a shoe to the ground. And that's when I knew I had officially become a Filipino badass.

My favorite act of badassery is passing unsuspecting motorists on the road. It's easy, really; you simply beep your horn twice without waiting for acknowledgement or reply, then pull into the oncoming lane and zoom by.

I love the looks of astonishment I get from the passengers in trikes and multi-cabs as I pass; My God, I can hear them thinking, here's a white man who's a badass too! Then they usually break into warm smiles, wave at me and yell hello.

Only one obstacle now separates me from complete mastery of true Filipino badass status: driving at night without lights. I shall try it soon. Only then, God willing, will I truly have arrived.

48
TANGLED LEGS

July 18, 2019

This morning I awoke with a foot in my mouth. It wasn't the first time—in fact, it's been happening for years. And all because of a Filipino custom to which I have forcibly adapted.

I'm speaking, of course, of the deeply held belief that children should share their parents' bed until, well, they have beds of their own. Which could happen after marriage. Or, as in my wife's case, when they finally take off for college.

The custom bears little resemblance to that of the US, where parents actually pride themselves on how quickly they can launch their little ones on the path to independence. I still have painful memories, for instance, of the sleepless nights I spent in a previous marriage listening to the woeful wails of my three-month-old daughter after consigning her to a room of her own.

"Geez, maybe I should go get her," I suggested imploringly to my then-wife, an American like me and the baby's mother.

"No," she said, "just let her cry and eventually she'll stop."

Eventually she did and, as far as we know, our little girl—now 35—hasn't turned out to be a serial killer.

In the Philippines it's different, something I should have detected immediately upon meeting the woman who now shares my bed. That was on Siargao Island, where—at her behest—we had hastily retreated to the house of her parents. Our first night together was a decidedly family affair with Ivy and her two sisters sharing the only bed, her parents and brother at its foot, and yours truly on the floor next to her, barely close enough to grab a hand. That, with some minor variations, describes our life ever since; the place previously occupied by her sisters now belongs to our eight-year-old son.

I realize, of course, that economics drives some of this. Unlike America, where average families occupy several bedrooms with an adjoining garage, in the Philippines, much larger families often, by necessity, sleep in one room. What's interesting, though, is how the custom persists even when the economics change; Ivy, from the moment our son was born, insisted on keeping him close.

For a while, I objected, setting a series of deadlines for our little boy's emancipation. But they always came and went. Then one day my wife said something that somehow struck a chord. "Honey," she said, "it's not like he's *always* going to want to sleep in our bed."

And so I let it be.

As you've probably guessed, the end of always has not yet arrived. To some extent, I've made peace with it. There are nights when I actually enjoy the little body between us, the warmth and comfort of our family togetherness. I have reluctantly learned to share the TV remote with our younger nightly companion. And on nights when the little guy falls asleep early, well, Ivy and I have perfected our own brand of intimacy by stealth.

But then there are those legs. Like a night-crawling spider, he can't seem to keep them organized, spreading the unruly appendages across the wide expanse of our nocturnal space. Sometimes it feels as if he has eight limbs rather than two; it's no wonder that his favorite character is Spiderman.

And so, this morning, I found that foot in my mouth. For a while, I lay in a sort of stupor, contemplating once again the sacrifices we make for love across the great divide of nations and cultures. Then, pulling those foreign toenails from the cavern in which they had found their comfort, I shoved them back toward my unconscious wife and turned away for a little more sleep.

Only ten more years until he leaves for college.

49
ALARM!

Aug. 22, 2019

The end of the world began with a burp.

It was 8 a.m. when the sound of the air conditioner belching air woke me up. Struggling with the first itchings of wakefulness, I rolled out of bed, walked to the veranda, and couldn't help but notice the large crackling fire raging within yards of our wall. It looked like it covered more than an acre and had already consumed many trees.

The surge of adrenaline that followed wasn't, in fact, the strongest I've ever experienced. That would be the time, years ago, that a bipolar girlfriend offended by my snoring poured a bucket of cold water over my head, forcing a rather immediate and jolting burst into consciousness. But the wall-licking brush fire was a very close second.

The only reason it didn't win the gold medal was because of the oddly relaxed attitudes of the dozen-or-so construction workers who had stopped building our house just long enough to enjoy the fiery spectacle.

"Hey, is this real?" I asked one of them, who responded with a shrug. "I mean, is it natural or controlled?" Another shrug.

"Has anyone called the fire department?" I finally wanted to know.

"Hm, *maybe*," he said, seeming a bit annoyed at the question.

Reflecting on it later, I realized that what I might have been witnessing was a classic display of *bahala na*, the well-documented Filipino attitude of fatalism that, roughly translated, means "whatever happens, happens."

That's not always a bad thing, mind you. In fact, it's one characteristic I love about Philippine culture; the calm acceptance of life's circumstances that are beyond our control. With a potentially devastating fire lapping at my gate, however, my obnoxious Americanism instinctively took over.

Cell signals are elusive at our house. And being the foreigner that I am, even if I had one, I'm not sure I'd know what to do with it. Fortunately, though—in this case, I'd say, *providentially*—we live next door to a coastal watch station manned 24/7 by Philippine Navy personnel equipped with, wait for it; complete regional and national communications capabilities, including radar, radio, satellite and, yes, cell phones.

There's even a story floating around that someone purporting to be from the National People's Army, a Communist rebel group with a local presence, once knocked on their door, threatening to blow up the facility's huge communications tower unless cash was immediately forthcoming. Within minutes, the story goes, armed soldiers surrounded the place, escorted the unfortunate would-be extortionist to jail, and later established a permanent neighborhood presence of their own. So, yeah, if I have to get hold of someone fast, the next-door neighbors are my go-to guys.

"Hey," I called over the wall opposite the one facing the flames, "have you guys seen this? Could you please make a call?" Several of them interrupted their texting long enough to take a gander at the encroaching conflagration which they apparently had not yet seen. Then one of them casually walked inside.

The rest is easy to tell; the fire department arrived within twenty minutes and, after some traipsing over the hills behind and around us, extinguished the blaze. And as so often happens, luck pitched in to help, in this case by shifting the wind's direction to blow the fire south up the hill instead of east toward our house. When the smoke finally cleared, it wasn't a moment too soon; the flames' licks had stopped just three meters outside our walls.

So, aside from an unusually exciting morning and grand cocktail party fare, what are the main takeaways? There are two: first, get a weed whacker to clear a swath around your property. Finally, never assume someone else will call the fire department when it's *your* house that's on fire.

50
MOVING DAY

Sept. 5, 2019

Like a lumbering turtle, the little house made its way slowly down the road.

To a casual observer, the sight was exquisitely startling; since when, I wondered on the verge of panic, do tiny houses have legs? Ahh, but this one did; in fact, over twenty! Had I fallen off a toadstool into Alice's wonderland? Had someone slipped hallucinogens into my tea? That's when I noticed that the legs all had bodies. And that's how I first learned of a curious Philippine custom called *bayanihan*, one of the odd but practical ways in which rural Filipinos express their community spirit.

"That tradition still exists?" a friend asked after I'd posted a picture of the house with many legs. A Filipina who'd grown up in the provinces, she later migrated to the city and now worked abroad. Though she had seen the tradition practiced during the 1960s and '70s "when I was young," my friend recalled, she'd never seen it in Surigao City and wasn't aware that it continued.

I am here to attest that it does. Only this wasn't a house, but a store.

We'd been told, of course, that city officials had asked our across-the-street neighbor to move his family's little *Sari Sari* store to make way for the concrete war memorial they were constructing just behind it. What we hadn't been told was just when, where, and *how* the move would be accomplished.

We now know the answer to that last question; by the combined muscle power of nearly two dozen friends and neighbors willing to spend a good portion of their day pitching in to help. The word *bayanihan* comes from the Filipino word "*bayan*" meaning nation, town, or community. And what it refers to is the traditional Filipino spirit of communal unity, work, and cooperation to achieve a common goal. Sometimes that involves moving a family's entire house—usually made of indigenous materials such as bamboo or nipa—to a new location, ordinarily in a remote provincial village. The most common method: carrying it on a set of bamboo poles. The distance is usually short and the home's foundations not so strong. Yet, to the uninitiated, the operation really resembles the movements of a lumbering turtle on a myriad of spindly legs.

So, what does all this mean? And why am I writing about it? Here's the thing; when you travel in expat circles, as I often do, you occasionally hear complaints regarding the alleged passivity of some Filipinos, the so-called attitude of *bahala na*, or "whatever happens, happens." One American friend, who has spent many years here, recently gave it an even more sinister spin.

"It's not only *bahala na*, as in never mind," he insisted, "but the more prevalent *bahal na ka* meaning never mind *you*. Sometimes people rise to the occasion to help, but mostly they just do whatever suits themselves and don't follow laws unless an enforcer is watching. The daily norm is *me* first."

I can't say that never happens. What I can say with some certainty, however, is that it wasn't happening on a recent moving day in Punta Bilar. Which is why I enjoy living here, where, with any luck, you can see a multi-legged *sari sari* store crawling like a lumbering turtle by the *mar*.

51
HEARTBEAT!

Sept. 19, 2019

Last week, I saw God in a parade.

It was the kickoff of an event I've chronicled before; the annual *Banok-Banok* street-dancing festival here in Surigao City. To be sure, the supreme deity didn't show himself immediately on that sultry Monday morning, but gradually and only by degree. Until, by parade's end, both an American visitor and I were literally watching the spectacle through tears.

"What an epic event!" remarked Ron Featheringill, a retired English professor with whom I've been close friends since high school. "It's like an epiphany; I may have to rethink my position on organized religion."

That, in fact, had been a major topic of conversation in the week since his arrival, with his wife, Bonnie, from California. Ron's position: that organized religion oppresses the masses by imposing a dogma, damning half of them to hell. Mine: that, while his assertion is demonstrably true, most Filipinos I know—though deeply religious—aren't highly dogmatic.

That's when we went to the parade.

It's designed to celebrate the lives and legends of the indigenous *Mamanwa* tribes, the original inhabitants of Surigao del Norte province. Long before any Catholics set foot in the Philippines, these people were hunting, gathering, and dancing to give thanks for their bountiful blessings. But the event also pays tribute to Saint Nicholas, the city's patron saint. Thus, anyone willing to get up early enough experiences a remarkable treat: watching bright-eyed young Filipinos in colorful native garb dancing their hearts out to the rhythmic beat of drums while swooning over statues of a

Catholic saint. The thing that stands out, though, is the unmistakable gleam of joy, reverence and, yes, even ecstasy, emanating from their faces.

"If this is what religion does," Ron said when it was all over, "then religion isn't so bad. It was very moving; it brought tears to my eyes, and I rarely cry. That people would do this in the name of religion is remarkable— even the devil would have been breathless."

As were we. This was the third time I'd seen the *Banok-Banok* parade and the second since moving to the Philippines. For me, it's always the same; gazing upon those smiling youthful faces stirs something deep inside. Is it the presence of God? Who knows? All I can say is that it is like the feeling I sometimes get while watching a beautiful sunset or admiring a placid blue sea. Certain pieces of music have the same effect, as do my favorite works of art, literary passages, and even cinematic scenes.

Not too long ago, my beloved wife sent me a surprise message bearing a heart-stopping image; that of a pregnancy test showing positive results. A few weeks later, standing next to her at an obstetrician's office in Cebu, we stared at a small screen as the grainy image from an ultrasound slowly took shape. There, unmistakably, lay a tiny arm stretched out above our baby's head. Then, as we both held our breaths, the air pulsated with the sound of a tiny heartbeat.

I knew then that God was in the room. Just as I did last week as the beat of *my* heart resonated to the pulse of those drums.

52
WHERE THERE'S SMOKE, THERE'S FIRE

Oct. 10, 2019

The stench was overpowering.

Curious as to its source, I stepped out onto the veranda. And there, for the second time in as many months, beheld a sky full of smoke. Much like the last time, it seemed to emanate from a large crackling brush fire feasting on a nearby hill. Unlike my previous encounter with deadly flames, however, these were across the street and seemed to be blowing *away*, rather than *toward* the house.

"Ivy, honey," I called to my wife inside, "can you come out here for a minute? What do you make of this?"

Shielding her eyes with her right hand, Ivy took in a sharp, smoky breath. "Looks like another fire," she said, stating the obvious. "Looks like it's out of control."

"Should we call the fire department?" I wondered aloud.

After a brief discussion, we decided not to, and for several reasons. First, no one else seemed overly concerned. Second, the fire was not threatening our house or, it appeared, anybody else's. And finally, having just summoned the local firefighters a few weeks earlier, we didn't want to wear out our welcome. Instead, we decided to send Ivy across the street for a chat with the residents in closest proximity to the blaze.

Half an hour later, she returned with an astounding tale. Our neighbors, she told me, had admitted to starting the fire with the intention of burning their trash. Then, when the conflagration escaped their grasp and began licking its way up the hill, they simply shrugged their shoulders and sat down to watch.

"What?" I gasped, "are you kidding? They told you all that?"

"I told them you are upset and concerned," she assured me. "They just laughed and said you must come from someplace that doesn't have fires."

In fact, I come from Southern California where the brush fires—or wildfires, as we like to call them—are frequent and devastating. Where, every few years, expensive homes get destroyed or sustain millions of dollars in damage, hundreds of acres of lush vegetation get wiped off the face of the earth and, occasionally, dozens of people die horrible deaths. Where, if you admitted to doing what our neighbors had just described, you'd probably end up in jail.

Ah, but this is the Philippines, where things are decidedly different. Where people see fires, at least in our rural neighborhood, as part of the natural order of things and consider fighting one not immediately threatening as an errand for fools.

And so the fire raged. Until, finally, it burned itself out, leaving a vast swath of charcoal black on a huge grassy hill once covered by green. I guess I can live with that. I suppose I have no choice. But it irks me that the neighbors who inadvertently scorched this once-lush patch of jungle appear to feel no shame.

There oughta be a law. Hey, wait, I think there is...

53
THE IMPORTANCE OF MEMORY

Oct. 17, 2019

The dust was so thick that you couldn't see the air. When it finally cleared, though, something remarkable came into view: thirty-five volunteers virtually sweeping away the grime of history.

The location was the newly constructed Battle of Surigao Strait Memorial and museum in Surigao City. The brooms? Well, they were there to prepare the place for its upcoming dedication at the annual commemoration of the great World War II battle that secured this nation's future.

It's an idyllic site, surrounded by lush green jungle overlooking the ocean at Mindanao's northernmost tip. It's also directly across the street from our house. And in the interest of full disclosure, let me just say that the committee overseeing the new facility recently named me its volunteer Public Information Officer, so don't look here for any critical coverage.

When we first visited the spot back in 2013, we were woefully ignorant of the location's grand history. All we saw then was an amazing view and all we heard was a quiet voice saying this was the place. And so, we bought it and started building our dream house.

It wasn't long, of course, before we began hearing other things as well, stories regarding the historic significance of the spot, considered the gateway to Mindanao. It was here in 1944, we learned, that the battleships of America and Japan engaged each other directly in a fierce and fate-changing fight.

In the end, Japan retreated badly beaten, turning the tide of war in the Pacific and paving the way for the eventual liberation of the Philippines. Casualties were heavy. And today historians describe the Battle of Surigao Strait as the final major naval battle in history.

During last year's commemoration at the nearby Lipata Ferry Terminal, the raising of those four nations' flags stirred me deeply. The keynote speaker was a man named David Mattiske, a then-93-year-old Australian veteran and one of the last surviving participants of the Battle of Surigao Strait. In a moving speech, he uttered the words now engraved on the new memorial's wall: "Let us pray that we never have another world war."

And that's when I realized the importance of memory. I'm of a generation that grew up in the shadow of World War II; my dad served as a merchant sailor aboard an American ship bound for Manila, and Mom was a German Jewish refugee who spent the war years in China. For many younger than myself, however, the war must be ancient history; a distant Game of Thrones played with complicated rules and objectives that now seem hazy.

I thought of that the other day as I watched a bevy of determined-looking people of several generations pushing brooms and planting caribou grass. They included officials of our own Barangay Punta Bilar, where the monument is located, volunteers from the local Philippine National Police, Coast Guard and Navy, Surigao City Dept. of Tourism representatives and a local chapter of the Girl Scouts. The scouts, in particular, grabbed my attention; for most of *them,* I'd wager, the only connection to World War II is that their great grandparents may have been alive when it happened.

Ahh, but this year—the great battle's 75th anniversary—there's something new to report besides the impressive-looking concrete structure overlooking the sea across from our house. The Japanese Embassy will send an official representative to take part in the dedication ceremony and help bring its message home. Somehow, I believe that would be welcome news to the brave men of all nations who fought and died here in that long-ago October morn.

54
THE BUZZ

Oct. 24, 2019

There was an unholy racket near my house the other night. Wait, I'm exaggerating; it was more like a buzz.

Buzzes, of course, are among those things in life often ill-defined. They can be terrible like, say, the buzz of a saw cutting through your knee or that of a bee headed toward your neck. Or they can be positive, like the buzz of good news.

The buzz I'm talking about was more like the latter; the buzz of excitement over something new in Surigao City. I didn't know that right away, of course. No, in order to find out, I had to venture across the street to the recently completed Battle of Surigao Strait Memorial.

As I've written before, it's a monument to the brave men of four nations—America, Australia, Japan, and the Philippines—who fought an epic naval battle there seventy-five years ago tomorrow. By *there*, I mean the wide expanse of ocean directly opposite the memorial and my house. By *tomorrow*, I mean October 25, when I will arise at 4 a.m. to honor the battle's dead.

My account of that experience will have to wait for a future column. Today, though, I want to tell you about that buzz; a noise, I don't mind saying, that honestly left me surprised. It's no exaggeration to say there were literally dozens of people coming and going from late afternoon until early evening. Being the inveterate reporter I am, of course, I couldn't resist walking down there to see what, exactly, the buzz was about. And what I saw was inspiring; entire families taking selfies in front of, well, a *memorial*.

"How do all these people know about this?" I asked City Mayor Ernesto U. Matugas, Jr. standing in the middle of the crowd sporting an enormous smile.

"Facebook," he said, and we both nodded knowingly.

The city's Supervising Tourism Operations Officer, Roselyn B. Merlin, was standing next to him. "It used to be so quiet here," she offered in a tone of commiseration, "but it won't be anymore."

"Yup," I said. "I guess we'll just have to adapt."

In fact, it's an adaptation I welcome, and here's why. In the roughly fifteen months since we moved to the Philippines, God only knows I've experienced lots of kindness and good will. I've also noticed at least one thing rather disturbing; the general lack of knowledge—or even interest—in history among the nation's youth.

The Philippines certainly doesn't have a monopoly on that; in my home country of the USA, I'm sure, there's at least as much ignorance and perhaps a lot more. But there I stood, watching teenagers—let me repeat, *teenagers*—gushing over a historical monument.

I'm guessing most of them know little about the battle it commemorates. The city built the monument in the shape of a ship heading north. Back astern sits a small museum full of artifacts from the battle. And on the front deck near the bow, perhaps where the bridge would be, four flagpoles stand proudly at attention, one for each nation that took part.

This morning, during what appeared to be a rehearsal for the big day, I saw those nation's flags hoisted aloft on these poles for the very first time. And as the sound of a solo trumpet playing taps wafted through my front door, I couldn't help but hope that those teenagers will come to understand what this monument is all about.

Even after the buzz has long since passed.

55
DRUM ROLLS

Nov. 31, 2019

It never gets old.

No matter how many times I hear the drum rolls, see the flags raised, marvel at the stirring national anthems, listen to the mournful sobs of a solo trumpet playing taps; no matter how many times I experience all that, the result is always the same.

Tears.

Not of hurt or pain. No, these are tears of appreciation, perhaps even love. They are tears of sadness, yes, but also tears of joy, as if those two seemingly opposite emotions can be one and the same.

It all happened at last week's 75th anniversary commemoration of the Battle of Surigao Strait. Two things were different about this year's annual commemoration. First, it took place at the newly inaugurated Battle of Surigao Strait Memorial, a beautiful construction overlooking the historic battle site in Surigao City. And second, a uniformed representative of the Japanese government sat on the dais next to his counterparts from the US, the Philippines, and Australia.

"We must never again repeat the devastation of war," said Cmdr. Michinori Fukuda, assistant defense attaché at the Japanese Embassy in Manila, looking utterly dashing in his starched white uniform. All the speakers shared that sentiment. And I realized how much can change with the passing of a generation.

My own closest association to World War II is through my mother, a German Jew who lost most of her family in the concentration camps of

Europe. The only way she survived was by emigrating to Shanghai, China, where she spent nearly a decade living in a refugee camp controlled—rather cruelly, she always said—by the occupying Japanese. So you can imagine how, growing up, well, let's just say Japan was not on my short-list of countries to be loved.

I thought about that last week sitting at the Japanese Cremation Site near what is now Surigao National High School, where Ivy was once a student. It is there the remains of some five hundred Japanese soldiers and navy personnel lie, many of them killed in the American bombings of 1944.

"Some fell on the battlefields worrying about the future of their homeland," Fukuda said, laying a wreath at a shrine erected to honor the dead. "Others perished in remote foreign countries after the war here."

Listening to the strange guttural chanting of a Buddhist prayer offered on their behalf, I couldn't help but reflect on how much these soldiers and sailors were like those of any other nation who perish in faraway places doing what they've been told. And it occurred to me then how right it was that someone from their country was here to grieve with us now. For only when former enemies can grieve together are they free to embrace a new future.

56
THE TRASHMAN IS HERE!

Nov. 14, 2019

It never fails.

Every week—usually, but not always, on a Wednesday, Thursday, or Friday—the sudden explosion of loud scratchy music from the street in front of our house startles us to attention. If it weren't so badly recorded it would, I'm sure, remind me of the local Carnation ice cream man of my childhood who customarily announced his presence with the gentle tinkling of bells or a raggedy musical jingle used only by him.

Alas, the weekly wake-up call in Punta Bilar isn't the ice cream man's but someone far more important though much less fun. Say hello to the Filipino trash collector who, if you ask him nicely, will stop by your house whenever he happens to pass. Just long enough for you to hustle your throwaways down to his truck, provided you move very fast.

In America, people take the weekly trash pickup for granted. On a scheduled day of the week (for us, it was always Monday) you simply leave your filled-to-the-brim plastic or metal trash container at the front curb and, like magic, its contents disappears. Here on the outskirts of Surigao City, it's not so easy. That's why, every Wednesday, Thursday or Friday, there's a tremendous hue and cry at our house, accompanied by urgent repeated chants of "The trash man's here, the trash man's here!!" Which usually, but not always, prompts the week's designated trash monitor to hustle down to the front gate dragging our fully loaded can.

We generally make it just in time though, sorry to say, sometimes we don't. It reminds me a lot of a scene in an old Steve Martin comedy called "The Jerk" in which Martin plays a semi-retarded (oops, I mean *intellectually disabled*) man who gets excited when the new phone book arrives. "The new phone book's here, the new phone book's here!!" he screams, to the utter bewilderment of all within earshot. "I'm *somebody* now!"

To most Americans, of course, the scene is hilarious because their new phone books arrive regularly without fanfare (although how long that will continue is a matter of some conjecture) and, well, having one's name and number listed in the phonebook is a matter of little consequence or note.

In my new hometown of Surigao, I doubt that most residents would even get the joke. The reason is obvious; people here have never received phone books, seldom have landlines, and even mail delivery is rare and unpredictable.

Which brings us to my central point; the difficulty of transitioning from an orderly and well-run society like America to one in which you get your electric bill from a neighbor who probably got it from the barangay captain, who got it from God-knows-where. A society in which, frankly, emergency services are unpredictable, mail delivery sparse, brownouts and water shortages common, and even trash collection a matter of some excitement and joy.

"Honey," my wife said during a recent heated discussion regarding inconvenience in the Philippines, "if you're going to live here, you've got to take it in stride."

And so I am trying. There are days when the best I can do is question my sanity (excuse me, *intellectual disability*) in deciding to move here. Then there are those others, the times in which a strange excitement wells up in my heart, a sort of primitive satisfaction that not everything happens just when and in the manner you expect. Ultimately, it's the raw alertness—a form of heightened consciousness, really—required in a world where one must fend for oneself rather than having all of his needs lined up in neat little rows.

It is at those times that I happily join the chorus of Filipino voices heralding the jagged and jarring unfolding of life. And it is then I cheer loudest for the celebrated coming of the trash man.

God willing, we will catch him in time.

57
FOR SALE BY OWNER

Nov. 21, 2019

The moment was both painful and revealing.

About a year earlier, my wife and I had purchased a 2012 Toyota Fortuner from her cousin in Butuan City. Now, finally, the completed title documents had arrived, and those sparkling wheels were legally ours. Excitedly, I ripped open the envelope, unfolded the first page, and gazed with expected pride at the spot where our names should have been. Then gasped in surprise, noticing immediately that only one name was there, and it certainly wasn't mine. This, despite the fact that I had specifically instructed the seller to include my name on the title.

The instructions were deliberate for a reason. As any expat living here knows, a foreigner cannot legally own land in the Philippines. If you're married to a Philippine citizen, you get a slight reprieve; your name can appear on the deed, though only as an afterthought. As in "property of so-and-so" (the citizen), "*married to so-and-so...*" (the dumb foreigner.)

As one of the many so-and-sos living here, therefore, I have carefully cultivated the habit of being extraordinarily kind to my Filipino wife. Mainly because I don't want to afford her even the hint of an excuse to put me out after sinking the bulk of my life savings into the house and lot we (excuse me, *she*) now own.

Ah, but cars are different; *anyone* can own a set of wheels, even foreign so-and-sos like me. So, it was a matter of token pride that the title of our *second* most valuable possession—namely the Fortuner—bear both her name and mine. The fact that someone hadn't considered the request important enough to honor was both painful and revealing. What it revealed is the mindset of many Filipinos regarding foreigners, i.e. that, though respected, they are, finally, only visitors. The painful part is that not owning land can sometimes translate into, well, not owning anything at all.

I completely understand the reasoning behind laws excluding foreigners from a piece of this earthly pie. For centuries, these islands were "owned" by colonialists from across the sea who'd simply seized them from their rightful Indigenous owners. So, it's not surprising that the first order of business after achieving independence was assuring the country remains in native hands.

Now that may be changing. Last week the House of Representatives' committee on constitutional amendments convened for a day-long hearing at Cagayan de Oro's University of Science and Technology of the Southern Philippines. Its purpose: to gather public input on various proposed changes to the country's charter, including the lifting of restrictions on direct foreign ownership to encourage international investment.

Let me state up front: I do not know whether that would, as hoped, create more jobs, income, and economic development for Filipinos. What I *can* tell you, though, is that it will certainly ease the minds of many expats who, like me, have married beautiful local women with whom they now live on parcels paid for by the sweat of their brows.

That said, let me also offer a bit of reassurance: the outcome will not affect how I treat my wife. I promise, whoever's name ends up on the title, to remain on my best behavior. Because, well, heck, you just never know.

58
FIRST COMMUNION

Nov. 28, 2019

The voices of children.

There's nothing quite like it, especially when they're raised in song. I had occasion to hear lots of children's voices singing over the weekend at my 9-year-old son's First Communion. What's remarkable is that it was also a first for me; my *first* First Communion.

That's because, though I live in an overwhelmingly Catholic country, I do not share that faith. In fact, I was born Jewish. And, though I have never been overly observant, I have always identified with Jewish culture, values, and certainly its superstitions. So, you can imagine the strangeness sometimes enveloping me at the dinner table when my son crosses himself and gives thanks to Jesus for the food he is about to eat.

I wasn't always open-minded regarding Catholicism. Though one of my best friends growing up was Catholic, I still cringe at the memory of his painful accusation that it was the Jews who killed Christ, a slander used to justify persecution throughout the centuries. Blaming Jews for the crucifixion, in fact, was Church doctrine until the mid-1960s, when the Second Vatican Council declared the real culprit to be "collective human sin," not just the Jews. And, anyway, most Filipinos I know—including my wife when I first met her—have only a vague notion of what a Jew is.

Still, it was with some apprehension that I approached the subject in my marriage, especially the issue of how to raise our children. In the end, I made peace with having Catholic kids for several reasons. First, my wife is more observant of her religion than I am of mine. Second, we now live in a

Catholic country where rabbis are few and far between. And, finally, the underlying values of Catholicism and Judaism are essentially the same.

I mean, Jesus *was* a Jew. And, aside from a few minor theological disagreements over whether he was the true Messiah, well, both religions teach charity, kindness, gratitude, and love; values any father would be happy to impart.

And so, it happened last Saturday that I found myself at Surigao City's San Nicolas De Tolentino Cathedral watching my son Isaac accept Jesus into his heart. The service was uniquely beautiful, with lots of processions, prayers and, as I mentioned, children's voices raised in song.

Isaac looked stunningly handsome in his black slacks, white shirt, and tiny bowtie.

My only discomfort came when the kids read aloud from the Gospel of John recounting the Jews "murmuring among themselves" after being told Jesus was the son of God. "Is not this Jesus, the Son of Joseph whose father and mother we know?" the Biblical skeptics allegedly asked. But even after Jesus corrected them, insisting he was indeed the "bread of life" and "he who comes to me shall not hunger," those troublesome Jews just kept on "murmuring and arguing among themselves."

Then Isaac brought us a little green card written in his childish scrawl, and I immediately forgave everything. "Dear Mom and Dad," it said, "I love you so much. I will never stop loving you."

I guess my feelings about religion are the same as some people's regarding gender, namely that it's fluid. Whatever religion my son identifies with is fine with me, on one condition; that he have a good heart.

To which I believe God Himself—whatever you call him—would have but one thing to add: *Amen.*

59
INVASION

Dec. 12, 2019

It looked like an invasion.

Dozens of young men marched past our house in long meandering lines, each cradling a rifle and decked in dark green military fatigues. The road they followed led to a pebble beach, then veered aimlessly off towards the mountains.

"Oh my," I said to Ivy, sitting next to me on our veranda, "I wonder what's going on?"

"They must be training," was all my wife could offer.

It wasn't until later we learned the invaders were not army soldiers, but officers of the Philippine National Police. And not just officers; they were members of the PNP's Special Action Force, an elite commando unit charged with battling terrorism and lawlessness nationwide. The same unit, I realized with a gush of respect, that lost forty-four members in an infamous 2015 ambush by Muslim extremists in Maguindanao, some five hundred kilometers south.

"Wow, now I'm *really* curious," I said. "Maybe I'll jump on the scooter first thing tomorrow to see if I can find them."

I couldn't. Despite a long meandering ride of my own through tiny adjacent barangays and ocean-side loops, the marching SAF guys were nowhere to be found. Perhaps this was a testament to their effectiveness, I thought. Perhaps they were hiding in plain sight. If so, I never saw them, so rode back home to enjoy a glass of *Tanduay* rum on the veranda I've already mentioned.

But the experience inspired reflection on living in a place where armed conflict is no stranger, a region considered dangerous by the rest of the world. Every time I visit my birthplace on the West Coast of the United States, in fact, someone invariably asks whether living in Mindanao is scary. My usual answer: no, I have never felt threatened.

To be completely honest, though, I've certainly heard stories of others who *have*. On the outskirts of Surigao City, Islamic extremists are few. But members of the armed revolutionary New People's Army are purportedly active in the hills near our house. One of my wife's relatives, a college student, told us she made friends with one at school. And though the NPA—military wing of the Communist Party of the Philippines—rarely targets civilians, the national police this week directed all units to be vigilant in the runup to the party's upcoming founding anniversary when atrocities frequently occur.

Short of atrocities, the revolutionaries have *other* distinctive ways of making their presence felt. Last year, for instance, friends living near those aforementioned hills told us they spent an entire day listening to the popping of gunfire not very far from their house. Thankfully, as far as we know, no one got injured or killed.

A well-known legend in our barangay, in fact, holds that a misbehaving foreigner living near here once received a visit from a local NPA delegation after threatening his neighbor with a gun. The community considered the guy a menace. Nobody but him and his interrogators know exactly what transpired during that solemn sit down, but the next day, the story goes, the unruly gunslinger opted to quietly leave the country for good.

And a Philippine Navy guy, one of several stationed 24/7 at the coastal watch station next door, told me someone claiming to be a communist revolutionary once showed up demanding cash for "protection."

"Sure," the Navy guy told him, "just let me go get the money."

Within minutes, military personnel had surrounded the place, holding guns to the would-be extortionist's head. And now that handful of Navy guys has the help of a contingent of armed soldiers charged with protecting everything in sight, including our house. Naturally, we've made friends with them and frequently have them over for dinner.

Here's the bottom line; the next time someone back home asks how I can keep living in "dangerous" Mindanao, I'll have a ready reply. "Why haven't you left California because of the earthquakes?" I'll fire back, or "what about all those mass shootings?"

Bad things happen everywhere, the best we can do is exercise caution and hope they don't happen to *us*. That said, though, it certainly doesn't hurt to have an armed military security squad living next door.

60
CRUELLY TORTURED PIGS

Dec. 19, 2019

I'll never forget the first time I heard it.

Ivy and I had just met, and she'd taken me home to see her parents. *Home* was a tiny thatched-roof village called Caridad on the eastern shore of Siargao Island. Mom and Dad had spent the day relentlessly interrogating me with the help of a few dozen relatives. Exhausted, we'd gone to bed early, only to be awakened the next morning by a series of blood-curdling screams.

Oh my God, I thought, Abu Sayyaf is cutting off someone's head!

In fact, I soon learned, it wasn't a friend's or relative's head on the block; the screams came from an enormous pig getting slaughtered on my behalf. And that evening, I experienced my first taste of *lechon;* the same animal that had so recently given up its ghost, now crispy and brown, laid out on the table with its flesh ripe for ripping.

The only thing missing was an apple in its mouth.

It's difficult to explain the impact of such a sight on the tender psyche of one for whom it is new. Difficult to explain, that is, to those who literally spend their lives within earshot of the final death squeals of cruelly tortured pigs. For a delicate soul like mine, though, the experience is akin to waking up, as a character in *The Godfather* did, with a bloody severed horse's head next to him in bed.

Back home, one buys pork at a supermarket clinically wrapped in cellophane. God forbid it resemble the animal from whence it came. More often than not, in fact, they freeze the meat to remove it even further from the distasteful circumstances of its origin.

For a time, I could almost forget the woeful sound of that dying pig's last anguished squeal. Living in the Philippines, naturally, I saw my fair share of whole roasted pigs resting on gaily decorated tables. Absent those piercing shrieks, I could somehow do the mental calisthenics necessary to convince myself that they were probably synthetic, perhaps made of rubber.

Then came my seventieth birthday.

It began, as I've said, with the harmonic caroling of sweet childish voices gently awakening me from my slumber. Then came a horrific contrast; the gut-wrenching squeals of terror from an innocent young pig being carried in a sack up our driveway to its slaughter. Holy Mother of God, I thought, it's happening again.

Try as I might, though, I couldn't resist following that jiggling bag all the way to the backyard where, as I watched fascinated, two neighbors unceremoniously dumped its contents onto an elevated board upon which the unfortunate animal's screeching throat was, even less ceremoniously, slit with a large gleaming knife. There was blood flowing every which way. And that's when I noticed my remarkable calm.

It wasn't exactly the calm that emanates from deep within, the kind that finds its strength in a firm belief that the universe is good and all things ultimately stem from some divine and everlasting core. No, this calm merely said *this too shall pass and you shall survive.* Unlike, I might add, that miserable pig. The calm that whispers a somewhat comforting message to the effect, more-or-less, that everything happens for a reason and it's all just part of life's flow. Which enabled me to face my next—and most recent— pig slaughtering with a newfound modicum of comfort.

That third little piggy, like its predecessor, also met eternity in our backyard, this time on the occasion of my son's ninth birthday. In fact, the event entailed a certain symmetry in that the tasty still-breathing hunk of pork hailed from Siargao Island, where I had first witnessed what it would soon experience. That's probably why I felt moved to record the poor creature's last night on earth with an artful photographic portrait.

I don't think I need to describe what happened next.

Here's the main takeaway; that there's actually some truth to our platitudes regarding life on this planet, specifically that living things are born and then they die. Pigs just do it sooner and in a more hideous fashion. And too, I suppose, one could say that—unlike us—their lives almost invariably serve an immediate and obvious purpose.

Filipinos understand all this. Unlike Westerners, who faint at the sight of blood, theirs is a culture with little tolerance for the luxury of flinching in the face of reality. To be honest, I'm liking that more and more.

61
PAJAMAS

Dec. 26, 2019

The situation was urgent.

Two young women recommended as potential housekeepers had arrived to be interviewed for the job. The problem was that it was 8:30 a.m.—two hours before their appointment—and I still lay in bed.

"Oh my God," I exclaimed to Ivy, who had appeared like an apparition at the bedroom door, "they're here already? Tell them to wait a minute and I'll be right down..."

I spent that minute surveying my closet. At T-Minus-10 seconds and counting, I shrugged my shoulders and decided. Then spent the bulk of that delinquent last minute grabbing my t-shirt and slipping a pair of jeans over my bunched-up pajamas. As I sauntered out the door, I could feel the material, usually so comforting in sleep, crawling up the skin of my legs like burgeoning boils under those way-too-tight jeans. It forced me to walk awkwardly, as if just learning how.

"Forgive me," I said to the pair seated with my wife at the dining room table. "So sorry to make you wait." They stared at me uncomprehendingly, which, I'm confident, was exactly how they were feeling. "OK," I said quickly, "let's have a talk."

And so we did.

Where I come from, there are only two reasons for getting caught in your pajamas. First, that you're a lazy bum who never takes them off because there's never any reason to. Second, that you're a filthy rich bum who never takes them off because there's never any reason to.

Hugh Hefner, the now-deceased former publisher of *Playboy Magazine*, made that second condition famous by insisting on always giving interviews wearing the same silk robe, pajamas, and slippers he lounged about in all day. That typically happened at the lavish Playboy Mansion in Chicago, which Hefner occupied for decades. The other things for which the mansion was famous—perhaps *infamous* is a better word—included the frequent star-studded parties the magazine magnate threw there, often dressed in that selfsame pajamas and robe.

As a young wannabe journalist, in fact, my most cherished ambition was to wangle an invitation to one of those parties which, I should probably mention, featured large teams of scantily clad women highly motivated to entertain. That invitation never came, though I did once land a brief interview with a low-level *Playboy* editor lasting just long enough for him to reject the story I was pitching.

For now, though, the point I'm trying to make is that, facing young potential hires in the Philippines many years later, I had no interest in impressing them either as 1/ a listless bum, or 2/ a listless wealthy foreigner. And so I'd pulled those tight little jeans up over my big, rumpled pajamas, causing myself to walk like a cripple. Thus, you can imagine my astonishment the following week on observing one of the same young women, now my employee, spending the day in her own brand of casual nighttime wear.

At first, I thought I was mistaken. It's still early, I figured, she'd just prepared breakfast and not yet had time to change. But as the day wore on and she continued performing her duties without the benefit of street clothes or, dare I suggest, the services of a toothbrush, well, I realized that my thinking might have to change. Several relatives in town confirmed that notion the following afternoon when, dropping by their house unexpectedly, we caught *them* wearing pajamas as well.

Could the culture be so different in this strange country I'd adopted with nary a thought regarding what I should wear? Was this daytime pajama-wearing routine truly a national phenomenon, or just a millennial thing? And, God forbid it was millennial, had the culture of my native America already arrived at the same conclusion?

None of these questions are immediately answerable. All, in fact, will require pondering. For now, though, let me just say that living in pajamas is a lot more comfortable.

So, while doing my research, I plan to adapt.

62
ADIRA

Jan. 3, 2020

Her name will be Adira.

In Hebrew, it means strong, noble, and powerful; all qualities I would wish to bestow on my new baby daughter set to arrive in just a few months. Twenty years ago, I would not have predicted my new fatherhood at 71. But here we are and here she will soon be, so predictions have morphed into planning and we're calling her Adira.

Back in 2008 when I married my beautiful Filipino wife, we talked about the possibility of this happening. Having already fathered two children in a previous marriage—a boy now 32 and a girl 35—I had no pressing need for more. But Ivy was still young and childless, and I recognized and embraced the importance of family in Pinoy culture. So I promised not to stand in her way and soon our beloved son, Isaac, was born. The second child was more difficult; after a series of miscarriages, we left it to God. Recently, it seems, He has spoken. Loudly. And so, barring some unforeseen shift in the winds of fate, young Isaac will soon have a baby sister.

He wasn't initially overjoyed at the news. "No," he insisted, "not a girl, a *boy!* A brother, not a *sister*." After some parental coaxing, his attitude softened somewhat until the other day, patting his mom's quite-ample tummy, Isaac told her he's eager for the baby to come out. He also expressed the hope for twins—a boy *and* a girl. It's a hope neither parent shares.

So what does our future hold? First off, of course, we'll be terribly busy for a while. Though less so, I suspect, than in the US where families stay scattered and unhelpful. Here in the Philippines, fortunately, we're likely to be surrounded by loving friends and relatives all eager to pitch in.

But there's a deeper meaning, and it has to do with roots. We arrived here nearly two years ago after more than a decade of living in the States. That's where our son was born and where Ivy built a career. It's also the place I spent my childhood and wherein my only remaining blood relatives live.

Our intention in coming to the Philippines was to make it our home. As any migrant will tell you, though, that takes a long time. For us, it began with finding a piece of land in a spot we loved and spending the next several years building the house of our dreams. There were lots of details to arrange; how to access our money and care for the things left behind. Not to mention getting the proper visa for me (both Ivy and Isaac are dual US/Philippine citizens), arranging for healthcare, buying furniture and, well, for Daddy and Isaac at least, adjusting to a culture that's brand spanking new.

But here's the thing; a house is not necessarily a home. Not until it reaches a certain marker; crosses an invisible, almost mystical, psychic line. For us, that line is the expected birth of our child in this strange land, the first member of our young family, after Ivy, more Filipino than American.

Shortly after moving into our house, we hung a single piece of art on its wall; a canvas mosaic depicting an American and Philippine flag merged into one. I suppose it represented our idealistic vision of what the future might hold. With the birth of Adira, that vision becomes real.

63
REVERENCE AND GRATITUDE

Feb. 2, 2020

It's all happened again.

The salutes. Proud words of praise. The dual bugles playing reverie; the gently bellowed national anthems; the prayers of reverence and gratitude.

As usual, I closed my eyes to imagine that infamous gray morning in 1944. And as usual, my heart swelled with emotions, belying the fact that those dark clouds rose well before I was born.

All this happened in memory of the historic Battle of Surigao Strait, in which the combined naval forces of the Philippines, America and Australia beat back those of Imperial Japan. The victory paved the way for the Philippines' liberation from an occupying power almost too fierce to defeat. It also occurred, as I've said, in the waters directly across from where my house now stands and where the raising and lowering of those four nations' colors has recently become a weekly ritual.

Which is why I've never hesitated to offer public condolences for the thousands of dead sailors now guarding my gates.

Most of them were Japanese. And the most poignant moment of the memorial celebration, for me anyway, came at a formal breakfast with some of their countrymen. Next to me sat my good friend, Ferdinand A. Almeda Jr., a noted historian, author, and the commemorative event's founder. And directly across from us: Col. Yu Nakano, defense attaché at the Japanese Embassy in Manila and his assistant, Cmdr. Takeharu Sekine.

"I make no excuses for Japan's actions during World War II," Sekine said during a heartfelt discussion on the lessons of history. "But I also know that those Japanese commanders slept soundly believing they were liberating Asia."

What he was saying, of course, was that they too were good men.

His comment reminded me of an enlightening experience I had in my youth. My mother was a German Jew whose entire family got murdered by the Nazis during the Holocaust. And, though born later in America, I once spent six months tracing my family's history in Germany.

It was around 1970 in Berlin that I met Klaus, a slightly older German artist, whose father—unbeknownst to me—had been an actual Nazi. As in, member of the National Socialist German Workers' Party. As in, one of the monsters responsible for the deaths of my forebears.

Klaus and I became fast friends. In fact, I ended up sleeping on the floor of the apartment he shared with his wife, Bridgette. Nights we used to stay up late drinking and carousing. And it was on one of those occasions that I noticed him weeping gently as he painted a picture of his father.

"This is what he looked like," Klaus said, proudly displaying the finished portrait. "He died of a heart attack when I was 10. This is the closest I've ever come to capturing his face. I finally got it right."

He pulled a handkerchief from his pocket and dabbed his eyes.

"You really loved your father, didn't you?" I said, laying a hand on my friend's shoulder.

"Very much," Klaus said. "I remember when he'd come home late, always on the nights the party met. How we used to worry; how we hugged him when he arrived."

"The party?" I inquired.

"Yes, the Nazi Party," Klaus said. "Dad was an old radical, didn't you know?"

Actually, I hadn't known until that moment. And so my friend forced me into an uncomfortable realization: that even Nazis had children who loved them.

The two Japanese military officers at breakfast in Surigao seemed fascinated by that story. And more interested yet in the news that my Jewish mother had somehow escaped Nazi Germany to spend most of the war years imprisoned in a refugee camp in Japanese-occupied Shanghai, China.

"Yes," Sekine said, his eyes slowly widening, "the Japanese were the only ones issuing visas to the Jews."

Conditions in a Japanese refugee camp must have been far from ideal. And yet I had to acknowledge an unassailable truth: that these men's invading ancestors had probably saved my mother's life.

And so, just as Klaus and I had done half-a-century before, the young Japanese defense attaché and his assistant broke bread. With a Filipino historian and an American-born newspaper columnist. To ponder— perhaps even relish—the terrifying ironies of war.

64
HIGH

Feb. 20, 2020

It was the electrical outlets that finally did it.

For a long time we waited for air conditioning, beds and, finally, comfortable mattresses. In the end, though, repositioning those outlets made all the difference. One obvious benefit, of course, was the ability to charge our cell phones within reach of our bed. The other; an opportunity to at last move into the top-floor master bedroom of what we like to call our newly constructed *mansionette* by the sea.

In a slight variation of Martin Luther King's famous "I Have a Dream" speech, we are (with apologies to the master) "home at last, home at last. Thank God almighty we are home at last." Last night, we slept upstairs. And now, in the immortal words of whoever said it, I am firmly convinced that "there's no place like home."

It's hard to describe the ebullience of finally feeling at one in your own domain. We spent the evening, innocently enough, watching TV from the bed in which we expect to spend much of the rest of our lives. Precisely on schedule came the requisite brownout, with its hour of darkness and silence. And then there was sleep, lovely sleep.

This morning I awoke with the smell of the sea in my nostrils and a deep green jungle at my back. Stepping out onto the upstairs balcony in a robe, I shielded my eyes to survey the motionless ocean stretching out before me all the way to southern Leyte. That's when I knew I had finally arrived.

I've said this before, and I'll say it again; I don't know how these things happen. I don't know why one man ends up starving while another lives in a big house overlooking Surigao Strait. Perhaps gratitude is the only appropriate response. Sitting on that balcony this morning, I felt something larger than myself. To that entity, whatever its name, I say thank you, thank you, thank you. Thank you for the New Year. Thank you for the blessing of this house. And thank you especially for the glorious hill on which it stands.

65
BLESSING

March 5, 2020

My only moment of uncertainty came when the priest sprinkled holy water onto our door.

There, mounted firmly inside the frame, hung a tiny Israeli scroll bearing Jewish prayers in clear Hebrew script. It was an important icon of my glimmering Jewish heritage; would the Catholic holy water make it hiss and explode? Would hot steam fill the room as the flames of Hell burned our new house to the ground?

Appreciating my anxiety requires some background. The scroll in question is called a *mezuzah*, a Hebrew word literally meaning "doorpost." A small vessel containing the *Shema Yisrael*, Judaism's most central prayer and declaration of faith, Jews traditionally attach it to the entrance of their homes in fulfillment of God's Biblical instruction to write "these words which I command you... on the doorposts of your house and on your gates." The concept: inviting the Lord into your home, to bless it and protect all who live under its roof.

Clearly not a bad idea, especially for a non-observant Jew such as myself living in a Catholic country with his Catholic wife and young Catholic-in-the-making son. Heck, there's even a future Catholic simmering, as we speak, in her mommy's growing womb. Hence my urgent determination to make things right with Moses and the Tribe.

When I say I'm non-observant, I don't mean unbelieving. I have what I consider a personal relationship with the deity, however one defines Him or Her. For me, it largely has to do with feeling something larger than myself;

an experience most pronounced, I'd say, in communion with life's miracles such as nature, art, kindness, heroism, or the birth of a child. Indeed, it is ultimately that presence which provides the joy, hope and, yes, love that propels me forward.

What I *don't* find lots of use for is the formal public ritual associated with much of organized religion, whatever its brand. So, though I identify as Jewish, it's more about culture and values than practice or belief. Which is why I have no problem allowing my children to be raised Catholic. And why I felt compelled to put a *mezuzah* in my house.

We did it ourselves, mainly because there wasn't a rabbi within seven hundred kilometers. After securing the artful Israeli-made mezuzah during a trip to the US last year, we simply instructed our favorite handyman to affix it to our door. Then, as he looked on in bewilderment, recited the Hebrew blessing conveniently downloaded from Wikipedia.

Ah, but now it was time to honor the *other* half of our mixed religious and cultural heritage; the traditional Catholic/Filipino blessing of a brand-new home. The event is essential in the Philippines, the chief attraction being the priest's blessing during which—after reciting the prayers—he makes a tour of the place, sprinkling holy water in every nook. Then you throw a big party for your family and friends featuring lots of *lechon* and— you guessed it–liquid comfort.

To get to the party, though, we had to first get past that door. As you may recall from your Bible studies, while relations between Judaism and Catholicism are fairly stable these days, there still is that ancient—and historically virulent—disagreement over whether Jesus is Lord. Whether, to be more specific, he's the True Messiah. Which is why it seemed prudent to hold my breath as the priest somberly prepared to administer his holy spray. Earlier I had pointed out and explained the significance of the tiny Jewish arc in the doorway, only to be met by his uncomprehending stares. Now I silently shut my eyes as the man in the white robe gingerly sprinkled his water on that blatantly unchristian doorpost.

A few seconds passed, and then... *nothing*. No hiss, no crackle, no fire, no tear; miracle upon miracle, our house was still there!

All of which leads me to conclude that God, whatever you call him, smiles upon our little union of culture, nation, and faith on this hilltop in Punta Bilar.

For which I must thank both Him and my lucky star.

66
ALIENS

March 19, 2020

It was the stuff of movies.

A large group of masked men sat stiffly in the stands of the local sports arena, staring blankly into space. In the photo, plastered across the front page, they looked like rebels captured in the heat of an insurgency now awaiting their appointments with death.

But these men were guilty of a far graver crime: appearing on the streets of Surigao without COVID masks. Their punishment: spending an entire day in silence with masks firmly affixed as a dire warning to others.

Like the atomic bombs ending World War II, the COVID pandemic has surprised the world overnight. One day, it seems, life was brimming with light and the next we were bound up in chains. If this were an actual movie, it would be a dystopian science fiction epic about invaders from outer space. As the deadly microbes descend, the world reacts by locking down its cities, closing its schools, confining people indoors, and banning all public gatherings.

Except, of course, those in locked sports arenas staged for the common good.

The Philippines seems to be taking it all seriously, imposing what's been described as one of the world's strictest lockdowns. A ring of armed guards, I'm told, surrounds Manila, charged with keeping insiders in and outsiders out. Crossing that grim barrier, not only in the capital but nationwide, requires a slew of documents signed by a myriad of public officials. And, of course, nothing gets approved without proper ID and a reason for travel deemed worthy.

Here in the province, infections are rare. And yet the city adheres to orders sent down from *Malacañang*, the national presidential palace. For starters, no one under 18 or over 65 may venture beyond their front door. As for the rest, well, the few actually employed may still go to work. But the rules allow only one person per household to leave once each day for food and other necessities, a trip facilitated by a special pass signifying the precise hour they may go. Our pass holder is Ivy's sister, Eva, who we now regard as the family Savior.

Already, there are rumblings of disaffection in other parts of the world. From what I hear, that's especially true in the US where history and tradition encourage rebellion. The Philippines has an alternate history, rife with colonialism and repression. The result: people here speak of annoyances only politely and in whispers.

I recently had a private conversation with several neighbors regarding the absurdity of closing every school in a province where not a single child has COVID. They all smiled and nodded in agreement, though I'm certain none would do so publicly.

The lockdown hasn't changed my own life much. Though I can't leave the house without official permission, that simply means more time for writing. And so I'm content to just sit and watch things unfold.

In fact, I see some cause for optimism. My adult daughter in Portland, Oregon, recently posted a note expressing thanks for what she characterized as a "much-needed time of rest and reflection." The lead paragraph of a recent story in the *Mindanao Gold Star Daily* reported that warring politicians in Cagayan de Oro and Misamis Oriental are coordinating actions against COVID. And last week—perish the thought—President Rodrigo Duterte declared a unilateral ceasefire with the armed Communist rebels of Mindanao to facilitate the unimpeded movement of supplies.

My heart bleeds for those everywhere who've become ill, died, or lost loved ones to this vile bug with no conscience. But the blood I'm bleeding is red, same as everyone else's. And maybe that's the lesson of this painful time; all of us bleed the same color.

Yesterday I saw a heartwarming post showing Italians, hit hard by the virus, singing to each other across a deserted street from the balconies to which they're confined. "Dear friends," a former colleague wrote, "come and weep with [us] as we embrace the joy, beauty—and glorious whimsy—of humanity."

And so I will try.

67
PARADISE RECLAIMED

July 9, 2020

The water was as crystal clear as I'd ever seen it.

Just beneath the surface, a swarm of green fish scurried about while scads of purple crabs crawled past each other on the rocks overhead. But the telltale sign was the smell; instead of sunscreen, the tidepool now exuded the natural odor of, yes, the teeming reef that God had intended.

I'm speaking of Siargao Island, specifically the famous rock pools of Magpupungko Beach which my wife and I visited recently after an absence of several months. We share lots of history with those pools. It was on their nearby shores that Ivy frolicked as a child and to which she first brought me after we met in 2006. And it is there that Ivy inherited a beautiful stretch of beach upon which we built cabins for our family and friends.

It was also there that we first questioned the efficacy of so-called progress.

That happened in 2018 after a dramatic series of events transformed the sleepy island into a tourist hotspot. First, a hit romantic comedy bearing its name opened in Manila. Then *Conde' Nast Traveler* named Siargao the best island destination in Asia, following up a year later by declaring it the best in the *world*. Finally, and perhaps most significantly, President Duterte ordered Boracay, the Philippines' then-reigning tourist mecca, closed for six months because of environmental concerns.

The results were immediate and astounding; nearly 200,000 foreign and domestic tourists—many diverted from Boracay—visited Siargao that year, a

50.7% increase from 2017. And the *Los Angeles Times*, my journalistic alma mater, commissioned me to write a 3,000-word feature for its front page.

The article I came up with tells a story both encouraging and sad. How the island's overnight transformation made struggling farmers into instant millionaires. How men who'd spent their lives catching fish now conducted island tours. And how a square meter of land once worth 400 pesos now sold for 75,000, sparking boundary disputes dividing neighbors in ways never seen. That point, in particular, hit close to home; by then, three legal challenges had targeted my wife's beach property, one of which is still pending.

Writing a major front-page feature for the *LA Times* takes some doing. After spending a week at the 2019 Siargao International Surfing tournament interviewing practically everyone on the island who could talk, I locked the door of my home office at Punta Bilar to organize my thoughts and write. Finally, after finishing the piece, I emailed it to Los Angeles, went through the rigorous editing process for which the paper is famous, and waited for my words to be published. Then the pandemic hit, and everything changed, including the premise of my story. Bottom line: the editors put it on indefinite hold and barangay health officials put *me* on indefinite lockdown.

The hold has proven more durable than the lockdown, which is how we finally got back to Siargao last week. And what we saw was truly amazing; the miraculous *re*transformation of an island that seems to have stepped backwards in time. Where once busloads of tourists arrived hourly, now lives a blissful silence. And crystalline rock pools recently inhabited by scads of multicolored bodies now offer solitary bathing under the ferry-like reflection of water dancing merrily on stone.

Naturally, there are economic changes as well. The erstwhile tour guides have all returned to their fish boats. And everywhere, one sees renewed evidence of the subsistence farming that has sustained this island for generations.

No one knows exactly when, or *if*, the tourists will return. And the locals have mixed feelings regarding whether that should even happen. "It's just like it used to be," one young man remarked wistfully, sitting at his family's restaurant near the entrance to Magpupungko. The diner is now closed, as are dozens of refreshment stands and souvenir shops lining the road to the beach. "Everything is so beautiful," he said, "but, of course, there's a lot less income."

Later, during a fiesta in the village of Ivy's birth, she remarked on how many people she recognized who'd returned home after absences of years. "It reminds me of when I was growing up," she said amidst the revelry of old friends drinking beer in the streets.

Then a passing police van with flashing red lights announced through a megaphone that it would soon clear the streets in observance of the 8 p.m. curfew. And, just like that, reality dragged our yearning souls unceremoniously forward from the mythic past to the uncertain future.

68
PREGNANCY IN THE TIME OF COVID

April 2, 2020

It didn't seem real.

That summed up my feelings about the new baby girl my wife is expecting. Until yesterday. That's when Ivy and I donned black facemasks for her monthly visit with the doctor, who reminded us that Isaac arrived after just 38 weeks. Ivy is now in her 37th week of pregnancy. So suddenly the imminent birth of our baby daughter seems more real than, well, this damned COVID-19 virus that forces us to wear those godawful masks.

In fact, we've been smiling politely at the jocular suggestions from some of our friends that we name the baby Covid. Truthfully, though, the proximity of those earthshaking events—the birth of our daughter and a terrifying global pandemic—has caused me disquiet.

"Hon, I'm a little worried," I'd been saying to my big-as-a-blimp wife, purposely downplaying the full tenor of my verging panic. "This is not the best time to be in a hospital."

What I didn't tell her was that the thought of her (or me) sharing space with sick people was causing my blood pressure to rise.

"Oh babe," she'd say sweetly, stabbing me with a single thrust of those same dark eyes that pierced my heart so long ago, "don't worry, I'll be fine."

Ivy, of course, is a professional medical technologist. So, were she not about to pop open like an overripe tomato, she'd probably be at some hospital anyway, staring those nasty little corona-causing cells into submission from the trigger end of a double-barreled microscope. What I'm saying is that my wife is the sort of person who's *accustomed* to wearing spacesuits to work.

"Sweety," she'd say, "honestly, everything will be ok."

Eventually, I just stopped asking.

Now, the doctor tells us, the only difference this little pandemic will make is that the hospital in which we had hoped to welcome our little Covid—err, *Adira*—is no longer available because suspected COVID patients occupy all of its spare rooms. Fortunately, we live in a province offering a plethora of medical facilities, leaving us with several other options.

Oh, and unlike Isaac's birth—which took place in America where doctors and nurses tolerate annoying hands-on husbands like flies in a barn—this time the authorities will not allow me to hang out in the delivery room to encourage my wife nor give critical advice to the attending physician.

"Don't worry," the doctor-in-question assured me yesterday, "we have an extremely comfortable waiting room where someone will keep you updated."

Which is nice, of course, but not quite the same. Oh well, guess if I can accept welcoming my child into a world under attack by killer microbes, I can adapt to not actually seeing her come through that door.

So where does all this leave us? Still, of course, just a little nervous. And excited. And *woefully unprepared*. Soon we'll have to interrupt this home quarantine to make a run for supplies.

Back in the US, recent newspaper articles have been imploring people not to hoard toilet paper. That isn't a problem in the Philippines where people seldom use that stuff at all. We'll soon find out whether that's also true of diapers.

69
READY OR NOT

April 9, 2020

My first moment of relief came with the request for measuring tape.

Before that, I literally paced the halls like nervous soon-to-be-fathers everywhere. "Is this your first?" a sympathetic nurse inquired kindly as I glided past his station.

"No," I mumbled through my tight-fitting facemask, "just the first time I'm not in the delivery room."

Actually, this was my *fourth* child, the first two being from a previous marriage. But they were born in the United States where annoying husbands may view the proceedings from inside the delivery room. Which meant that I was too focused on keeping my lunch down—especially during the most recent delivery performed by Caesarian section—to be pacing any halls.

Until now.

This experience was unique in three major ways. First, we were in the Philippines which, again, has less tolerance for the emotional needs of bothersome husbands. Second, this was a *planned* C-section chosen by us to avoid the painful 24-hour labor of the past and opt for a quick tubal ligation in the bargain. And, finally, we were in the middle of the COVID-19 pandemic during which, I'm told, even many otherwise liberal hospitals in the US are closing their birthing rooms to anyone deemed nonessential.

So there I was, pacing the halls, when a nurse came out for that measuring tape. Whoa, I thought, they finally have something to measure.

A few minutes later, I could hear the muffled-but-unmistakable cries of a baby from behind those thick double doors. Then suddenly another masked nurse came out holding a white towel bearing—wait, two bloody red globs of flesh? Oh my God, I thought, is this all that's left of the mother?

Sensing my distress, the nurse spoke quickly. "These are your wife's fallopian tubes," he explained. "We took them out, so she won't have any more babies."

This was no surprise, of course; having her tubes tied had been a mutual decision. And yet, despite all that, I couldn't help but feel a momentary pang of regret as I gazed down at what remained of Ivy's reproductive capacity. It disappeared quickly, however, as almost immediately those great double doors swung open a third time and out pranced yet another nurse, holding our screaming little ninny.

"Congratulations Mr. Haldane," she said, just like in the movies, "you have a healthy baby girl." Like every parent who's ever lived, of course, my immediate reaction was that she was the most beautiful thing I'd ever seen. My only regret then was that the bothersome anti-coronavirus mask stuck to my face was hiding the width and depth of my smile.

As is the custom in the Philippines, I spent the next several nights—the duration of my now-somewhat-lighter wife's hospital stay—sleeping on a cot next to her bed. As is *my* custom, I also took a moment to bond with my new baby daughter.

Holding her in my arms, staring into that round little face with half-closed eyes the color of her mom's, I experienced the familiar moment of wonder I have felt with each of my four children. It is hard to describe, but let me just try. It's the closest I've ever come to eternity; that bittersweet moment of awe at the miracle of life itself, the wondrous ways God and nature embrace to create the unimaginable and renew it again and again.

A good thing to hang onto in these dark and dangerous times.

I'm no fool; I understand I will be 89 by the time my daughter graduates from high school. Her college education will probably take me well into my

90s, and on her wedding day, I'll probably be in a wheelchair as she rolls me down the aisle.

I plan to be there for all of it. As I've already told my wife, each new child adds twenty years to my life. So far she's skeptical, but, as I've said, I aim to prove that it's true. In fact, now that I think about it, I *am* sorry that we threw away those bloody fallopian tubes.

If we still had them, I believe I could live forever.

70
TRAIN TO BUTUAN

Aug. 20, 2020

I know, I know; it wasn't a train but a car, and we weren't in South Korea but the Philippines.

That said, however, there are striking similarities between Isaac's favorite movie, *Train to Busan*, and our recent drive to Butuan; both involve monsters. In the movie, they are packs of zombies who murder most of the passengers before they ever get to South Korea's second-largest city. On *our* drive, the monsters were more like vampires; strange beings wearing long surgical coats and facemasks who poked us with needles to suck out our blood.

Before you send hate mail, let me just clarify that I am not calling the nation's COVID frontliners monsters. I understand that they are mere human beings–perhaps braver than most–charged with keeping all of us healthy. And that, in our home province of Surigao del Norte, part of that job requires drawing blood from all incoming traffic for mandatory COVID rapid tests.

Wait, before going any further, let me set the scene. See, we needed to get our new baby, Adira, a Philippine passport, both for identification and, eventually, travel. The closest place to accomplish that was Butuan, a neighboring province two-and-a-half-hours south of Surigao City. We had heard, of course, of the COVID checkpoints guarding all provincial boundaries but didn't imagine they would pose a problem. So after spending a day-and-a-half gathering the clearances and signatures required, we departed for what purported to be a pleasant six-hour journey.

No, I promise you that calling those frontline medical workers monsters was just a literary device to make the opening of this column funny. Ha, ha, ha. Well, here's where the humor ends: on the way back, the baby tested positive. Which surprised us given her tender age and limited—or should I say *nonexistent*—experience beyond the presence of her parents. Both of whom, incidentally, tested negative.

"What?" I stammered upon hearing the news. "Wait... what?"

No worries, though. The heroic frontliners under the roadside tent at Caraga Regional Hospital's Bad-as (I swear that's what it's called) Health Center had a ready solution: fourteen days of institutional quarantine for both the baby and her mother.

"What?" I repeated in case they'd missed it the first time.

Perhaps I should pause here to comment on how easily fractured are our illusions regarding the actually quite-fragile emotional state in which we all are living. I mean, one minute you're a happy family excited about getting home to binge watch *Grey's Anatomy*, and the next... well, the next minute you're trapped in a dystopian science fiction novel as one of the godawful scary aliens that authorities have, thankfully, just captured.

"Hey waitaminute," I said, as if there was any other choice.

So I focused on quelling the rising panic in my gut while Ivy spoke *Bisaya* to a doctor on the phone because, hey, it wouldn't be safe for them to talk in person. That's when I remembered reading somewhere that these so-called "rapid tests" have an 80% false positive outcome.

So we argued, pleaded, and cajoled. And miraculously persuaded them to give our baby another test. Which, unsurprisingly, came back negative.

Well, OK, they told us, that's a slightly different story. But not until after a guided tour of the so-called "COVID ward" where Ivy and the baby would ostensibly be staying. To my untrained eyes, it looked like a temporary structure equipped with makeshift beds separated by paper-thin curtains, affording excellent exposure to the virus. "Hey waitaminute," I said for about the zillionth time.

Eventually, they dutifully reported the positive—but not the negative—result to the health officials in our home barangay. Which is why, upon arrival, those same health officials quarantined us for fourteen days, but mercifully in our house rather than at some foul-smelling virus-oozing ward. They even placed a yellow "caution" tape around the property's perimeters to warn away our neighbors. And now every morning a squad of strangers in spacesuits comes by to take our temperatures, ask how we're feeling, and post our pictures on Facebook.

At first it upset me, but then I read the pre-test document they made us sign before re-entering the province. "If the test results turn out NEGATIVE," the paper says, "I agree to be placed under quarantine for at least 14 days at any of the Provincial/City/Municipal/Barangay Quarantine Facilities/Isolation Units in the Province of Surigao del Norte. If the test result is POSITIVE," it went on, "I *strongly* (italics added) agree."

So, given the circumstances, we seem to have gotten off easy. And guess what? We've become veritable *Grey's Anatomy* fanatics.

71
SCHOOL DAZE

July 16, 2020

It was as if a giant buzz saw had occupied the house.

The walls vibrated, and the floors rumbled. The surrounding air pulsated with a rhythmic pounding in direct opposition to the beating of our hearts. And in the upper regions of our heads containing eardrums, the soul-thumping disruptions were truly profound.

The worst of it was that the clock read 6 a.m.

So, grumbling into the morning dimness, I rolled painfully out of bed and stumbled downstairs. There to find Isaac and his cousin dancing their little hearts out to the bashing beat of, yes, *TikTok* on an enormous TV screen.

"Hey!" I yelled as loudly as I could, "would you mind turning that down?" It took three repetitions just to penetrate their prancing ears. Welcome to the brave new world of navigating a pandemic with kids.

Back in the pre-COVID era, the sounds of preparing for school usually permeated this time of day; the boys would take their showers while my son's *tita* packed their lunches. Later, after serving breakfast and dressing the children, she'd hustle them into the family van for a school drop off en route to work.

Then the coronavirus struck and transformed our lives. For a while we tried online learning, with disastrous results. Finally, President Duterte announced no schools would reopen until there's a vaccine. "Unless I am sure that they are really safe," he declared, "it's useless to be talking about... classes."

Fortunately, both Isaac and his mom are dual US/Philippine citizens, which gives us other options. So, as the traditional first day of school approaches, we face a daunting decision; whether to go there or stay here.

In some ways, it's surprising that real-time schooling in the Philippines is on hold, at least in the town where we live. While thousands have tested positive nationally, only a handful were in Surigao City, none of whom died. And here's another thing; there still isn't a child among them. Yet Filipinos, especially in Manila and Cebu, have endured what one foreign newspaper recently described as "the world's longest and strictest coronavirus lockdown."

Contrast that to the United States where, despite winning the global competition for the highest number of infections, the idea of wearing masks, staying home, and socially distancing has literally inspired protests and shouting matches nationwide.

Part of the difference lies in culture. Having lived under Spanish–and later American–colonial rule for nearly 400 years, Filipinos are not unfamiliar with following directives from above. Besides which, they live in an Asian-influenced culture that emphasizes family and community interests over individual concerns.

Compare that to Americans, who are individualistic, opinionated, ornery, and obnoxious. I should know because, heck, I *am* one. Which contributes to our present dilemma; to go or not to go.

The decision on whether to open schools in the US ultimately rests with each local school district. While several large districts–including Los Angeles and San Diego–recently announced that, for the time being anyway, their brick-and-mortar facilities would remain closed, we have yet to hear from some of the smaller rural districts, including the one we left behind. Other factors will also weigh in on our decision; the levels and locations of lockdowns in the Philippines, availability of tickets and flights, and how soon we receive our new baby's passport.

None of which we yet know. Or, put another way, we have absolutely no idea of what we're doing.

Fear not, though, we are using this precious time excellently; hunkered down and enjoying ourselves, we are watching lots of movies, eating scrumptious meals and, well, even learning new skills.

Take me, for instance; I am fast becoming an accomplished dancer on *TikTok*.

72
LIBERATION

May 28, 2020

It seemed like a simple suggestion.

"Hey hon," my wife said, "let's take a walk before dinner." So we did, and in that walk lay our salvation.

It's not like these are ordinary times. In fact, it had been eight weeks since I'd left the house and then only for the sterile environment of a hospital hallway to await the birth of our daughter. I would have said that was the middle of this damnable COVID quarantine, but now it seems like only the beginning.

"Should I take my mask?" I asked.

"We're just walking down to the beach," she said, "but why don't you take it in case?"

The route was familiar; out the front door, down the driveway, out the gate, and then a hard left. For a while, we walked uphill, pausing occasionally for breath as Isaac and his cousin pranced jauntily ahead. It was an unusually humid day, even for the Philippines, and standing on the pavement, I literally mopped the sweat off my brow as Ivy comforted the baby resting snugly on her chest.

"This is her first walk," she reminded me, emphasizing the historic significance of the day.

I paused only an instant before formulating a reply. "Mine too," I said, and with that we moved on.

Forgive me, but the rest of the story stubbornly insists on writing itself. I have argued, but it won't budge, so here's this story's own telling:

The pebbles on the beach had been polished by the surf. The only other people there were fishermen by birth. And as I watched our little boys just playing in the sun, I thought of what we'd all been through and just how far we'd come.

As the great sickness bore down on us, we'd cowered in our homes, too nervous to come out and clearly frightened to our bones. Some had stayed inside for months, just staring at a screen. Others emerged only with masks, concerned that they stay clean.

And yet the sun had shown its face, still shining and so nice. How majestic its reflection looked, sparkling on water like ice. It seemed as thin as ice is too, as if you could cross it in a canoe. But beneath that ice lay a great vast stillness, the kind that calms one's soul. And firmly anchors it to earth, like a deeply rooted pole.

Later, when we got back home, a housemate manned the gate. He told us that the police were out, and we better not be late.

I don't know when I'll return, perhaps not for a while. However long it takes me, though, please know that I will smile. Because now I've seen the sea, the sun, and the smoothness of that stone. And however long I have to wait, the ocean will atone.

73
ADIRA IN THE MORNING

Dec. 31, 2020

A gentle tapping on the shoulder.

That's how my mornings begin in these uncertain times. Eventually, I open my eyes. And behold the radiant smile of my 9-month-old daughter, Adira, welcoming me to a brand-new day. Just as we so recently welcomed her.

When that magical welcoming arrived, I remember arising transfixed. Holding the new baby in my arms, I experienced, as I told you then, the familiar moment of wonder I have felt with each of my four children. "It's the closest I've ever come to the sensation of eternity," I wrote. "A bittersweet instant of awe at the miracle of life itself—the wondrous ways in which God and nature hold hands to create the unimaginable and renew it again and again."

The days since then have passed quickly. Adira has learned to crawl and raise her hands in the crude imitation of a wave. And her dietary habits have developed nicely; besides the ubiquitous mother's milk, she now consumes soft cereal and crackers with a determination that inspires.

But the baby's most fetching feature by far is her smile; a toothy, wide-open grin that melts my heart every time. She seems to exhibit it most generously on those mornings when, in true Filipino fashion, she awakens with her family all slumbering in the same bed. Then, squealing with delight, explores my teeth like some probing future dentist or strokes my beard as if it were a thing of genuine wonder.

And that's when I realize that, to Adira, *everything* is truly wondrous because everything is new. And I'm struck again by the many ways she's taught me to see the world through her eyes.

All of which seems especially relevant on this cusp of a New Year. The one just past was terrible; many died, and the rest lived in hiding and in fear. And yet, for us, 2020 also saw the birth of a new child and, with her, new hope.

I thought about that recently while listening to the choir of Michigan's renowned Hillsdale College singing *O Holy Night*:

"A Thrill of hope,
The weary world rejoices,
For yonder breaks a new,
And glorious morn."

And so, I hope, shall it be for us all.

ACKNOWLEDGMENTS

First, I want to thank everyone, known and unknown, whose lives and experience became fodder for my pen. Some of you know who you are, while others may not. I also wish the thank the readers of my column, both in the newspaper and elsewhere, whose comments and feedback inspired thoughtfulness and courage. Special thanks to my good friend, Fernando A. Almeda Jr., author of *The History of a Province: Surigao Across the Years*, who hooked me up with the *Mindanao Gold Star Daily* where my weekly column still appears. Also, to that newspaper's former editor, Herbie Gomez, who gave free rein to my whims, and its current editorial leader, Cong Corrales, who continues in that vein. To Dr. Neal Rana and Jake Miranda for providing front-and back-cover photos. Finally, a heartfelt thanks to my editor, Adina Morgan, whose feedback and suggestions were invaluable.

ABOUT THE AUTHOR

David Haldane, a former *Los Angeles Times* staff writer, has published two previous books: the award-winning memoir, *Nazis & Nudists*, and a short-story collection called *Jenny on the Street*. In addition to his journalism, essays, and short fiction, Haldane has written and produced radio features for which he was awarded a Golden Mike for excellence by the Radio & Television News Association of Southern California.

Haldane, along with his wife and two young children, currently divides his time between homes in Joshua Tree, California, and Northern Mindanao, Philippines, where he writes a weekly column for the *Mindanao Gold Star Daily*.

NOTE FROM THE AUTHOR

Word-of-mouth is crucial for any author to succeed. If you enjoyed *A Tooth in My Popsicle*, please leave a review online—anywhere you are able. Even if it's just a sentence or two. It would make all the difference and would be very much appreciated.

Thanks!
David Haldane

We hope you enjoyed reading this title from:

www.blackrosewriting.com

Subscribe to our mailing list – *The Rosevine* – and receive **FREE** books, daily deals, and stay current with news about upcoming releases and our hottest authors.
Scan the QR code below to sign up.

Already a subscriber? Please accept a sincere thank you for being a fan of Black Rose Writing authors.

View other Black Rose Writing titles at
www.blackrosewriting.com/books and use promo code
PRINT to receive a **20% discount** when purchasing.

Made in the USA
Las Vegas, NV
16 March 2023

69216626R00098